A Course of Study in LATIN & GREEK WORD ROOTS

SOUND
- symphony
- euphony
- cacophony

DOWN
- denounce
- despondent
- debilitate

UNDER
- subversive
- subliminal
- subordinate

SPEAK
- elocution
- colloquial
- loquacious

QUICKLY IMPROVE:
High School Students' Vocabulary for College.
College Students' Vocabulary.
Academic Vocabulary.
General Vocabulary.
Test Performance; GRE, SAT.

INCLUDES:
- Twenty-Five Lessons.
- 375 Academic and Important General Vocabulary Words.
- Definitions and Lesson Quizzes.
- Brain-Efficient Pattern Charts To Make Learning Easier, Faster, and More Enjoyable.

For High School & College Students

Matthew Glavach, Ph.D.   Zoe Gillespie, B.S.

GLAVACH & ASSOCIATES

Copyright 2020, Matthew Glavach, Ph.D.

Latin and Greek Word Roots, H.S. /College

Teacher Guide

Contents ... 2 Introduction ... 3 Answer Keys ... 111

Program Lessons

1. Word Roots	logy, ology (study of)		6
2. Word Roots	graph, graphy (writing, written, recording)		10
3. Word Roots	e, ex (out), extra (outside, beyond)		14
4. Word Roots	a, an, il, im, in, ir (not, without)		18
5. Word Roots	pre (before), pro (before, forward), post (after)		22
6. Word Roots	de (down), sub (under, below), super (above, beyond)		26
7. Word Roots	ceed, cede (to go, yield), duc (lead, take), clud, clus (close)		30
8. Word Roots	dia (through, across), trans (through)		34
9. Word Roots	sym, syn (same, together), co, con (with, together)		38
10. Word Roots	spec (look, see), vis, vid, scop (see, view)		42
11. Word Roots	circum, per/i (around), centr (center)		46
12. Word Roots	ben/e, bon, eu (good, well)		50
13. Word Roots	mal (bad, hate), mis/o (hate), dys (bad, impaired)		54
14. Word Roots	nom, nym (name, word), neo, nov (new)		58
15. Word Roots	scrib, script (to write), graph/y (write, writing)		62
16. Word Roots	lingu (language, tongue), log (word, discourse), liter (letters)		66
17. Word Roots	dict, locu, loqu (to speak)		70
18. Word Roots	phon (sound), voc (to call, voice)		74
19. Word Roots	phil (love), fobia (fear), fab (speak)		78
20. Word Roots	bi/o (life), viv/i (life)		82
21. Word Root	gen (birth, race, origin, kind)		86
22. Word Roots	ped, pod (foot, feet), ped (child)		90
23. Word Roots	arch, cracy (govern), arch, prot/o (chief, first)		94
24. Word Root	de (down, away, put off way)		98
25. Word Roots	di, dis (not, apart)		102
Final Examination			106

Copyright 2020, Matthew Glavach, Ph.D.

INTRODUCTION

A Course of Study in Latin and Greek Word Roots, Program 3, includes 375 academic and important general vocabulary words. It is designed to quickly improve high school and college students' vocabulary, both academic and general vocabulary, and to improve performance on tests such as the GRE and SAT.

Program Organization

The program has two parts.

Part 1 has twenty-five lessons. Each lesson has four pages and includes the same activity sequence. The consistent lesson design makes it easy for the teacher to administer and for students to follow.

Page 6 presents the fifteen words for the lesson.
Page 7 presents the lesson words in a chart that includes the Latin and Greek word roots.
Page 8 is the study card with the word definitions and examples.
Page 9 is the lesson quiz.
Part 2 is the Final Examination.

Presentation

(ON THE CHALKBOARD, WRITE THE WORD (**biology**).

bio**logy**

(READ TO STUDENTS.)

An easy way to figure out the meanings of many words is by knowing the Latin and Greek word roots. Look at the word ***biology***.

bio means *life,* and **logy** means ***study of***.
biology means ***the study of life.***

Word roots are the parts of words that carry the meanings. Latin and Greek word roots make up approximately sixty percent of the words in English text. Knowing Latin and Greek word roots makes it possible to expand your vocabulary easily because the word roots have consistent meanings that are found in many words. Most aptitude tests are tests of vocabulary. Students with the best vocabularies do well on these tests.

NOTE: In words with Latin and Greek roots, the roots often provide the meaning. In some words, they provide hints to the meaning; so, it is important to think about your knowledge of the word along with the word roots.

Student Notebooks

Students complete their work in individual notebooks. The notebooks should be organized in the following way.

First Lesson Page (page 6). Word Presentation

This page can be used for writing words for spelling practice but is optional.

Second Lesson Page. (Page 7) Latin and Greek Word Root Chart. This page also includes the third lesson page (page 8), Study Cards.

This page should look like the example below and include lines for all 15 words.

LESSON ONE

Word 1: biology   (Students write the lesson words.)

Student Definition   (Based on word roots and student knowledge of the word.)

_____

Study Card Definition

_____

Word 2: exobiology

Student Definition

_____

Study Card Definition

_____

Word 3: ecology

Student Definition

_____

Study Card Definition

_____

Word 4: _____

Student Definition

_____

Study Card Definition

_____

Word 5: _____

Student Definition

_____

Study Card Definition

_____

Continue to include all 15 words. (Students keep their work for all lessons in their notebooks.)

Copyright 2020, Matthew Glavach, Ph.D.

Third Lesson Page. (page 8) Study Cards. The study cards have definitions and many sample sentences and examples.

Fourth Lesson Page. (page 9) Lesson Quiz. The lesson quiz includes matching words to definitions and matching word roots to words.

Completing Lesson 1

Lesson Page 1. Word Presentation

The first page is a chart of the 15 words for the lesson. The words are presented with a focus on the key word roots (bold type).

Each word should be pronounced, and students should practice pronouncing each word. Point out the similarities in the word groups. (bold type). Tell students that they will be studying the Latin and Greek word roots that make up the words on the next page. If students need spelling practice, they can write the words. (This page can also be used for practice before taking the lesson test by having students circle the word roots and then having them practice discussing the meanings of the roots and the words).

Lesson Page 2. Latin and Greek Word Root Chart

This page has the lesson words and the Latin and Greek word roots in a chart. Students use the word roots to help them with their own definitions.

(1.) The students write the word and their own definition on the first line in their notebooks.

(2.) They write the study card definitions (from the on the second line in their notebooks.

Typically, they write the definitions and not the sample sentences and examples.

There are five words in each lesson part. Depending on students' word knowledge, one or more lesson parts can be presented in an instructional period.

Lesson Page 3. Word Study Cards

The word study cards have definitions, sample sentences and examples. Students use the cards to write the definitions in their notebooks. Activities such as writing original sentences for certain words, locating synonyms and antonyms, completing drawings of interesting words can also be included.

Lesson Page 4. Lesson Quiz

The lesson quiz has two parts. In part one, students write the word for the definition and in part two they write the word root for the word. The words and the word root meanings should be reviewed prior to completing the test. The first lesson page can be used for this activity. Students can circle word roots and discuss word root and word meanings.

Final Examination. Thirteen matching tests based on lessons one through twenty-five.

bio**logy**
exobio**logy**
eco**logy**
etio**logy**
geo**logy**

astro**logy**
genea**logy**
zo**logy**
chron**logy**
psych**ology**

cosm**ology**
audi**ology**
ethn**ology**
anthrop**ology**
paleoanthrop**ology**

PART 1 — STUDY OF

- LIFE → **bio**logy
- OUTSIDE — exo**bio**logy
- ENVIRONMENT — **eco**logy
- CAUSE — **etio**logy
- EARTH — **geo**logy

LESSON 1

logy
ology
STUDY OF

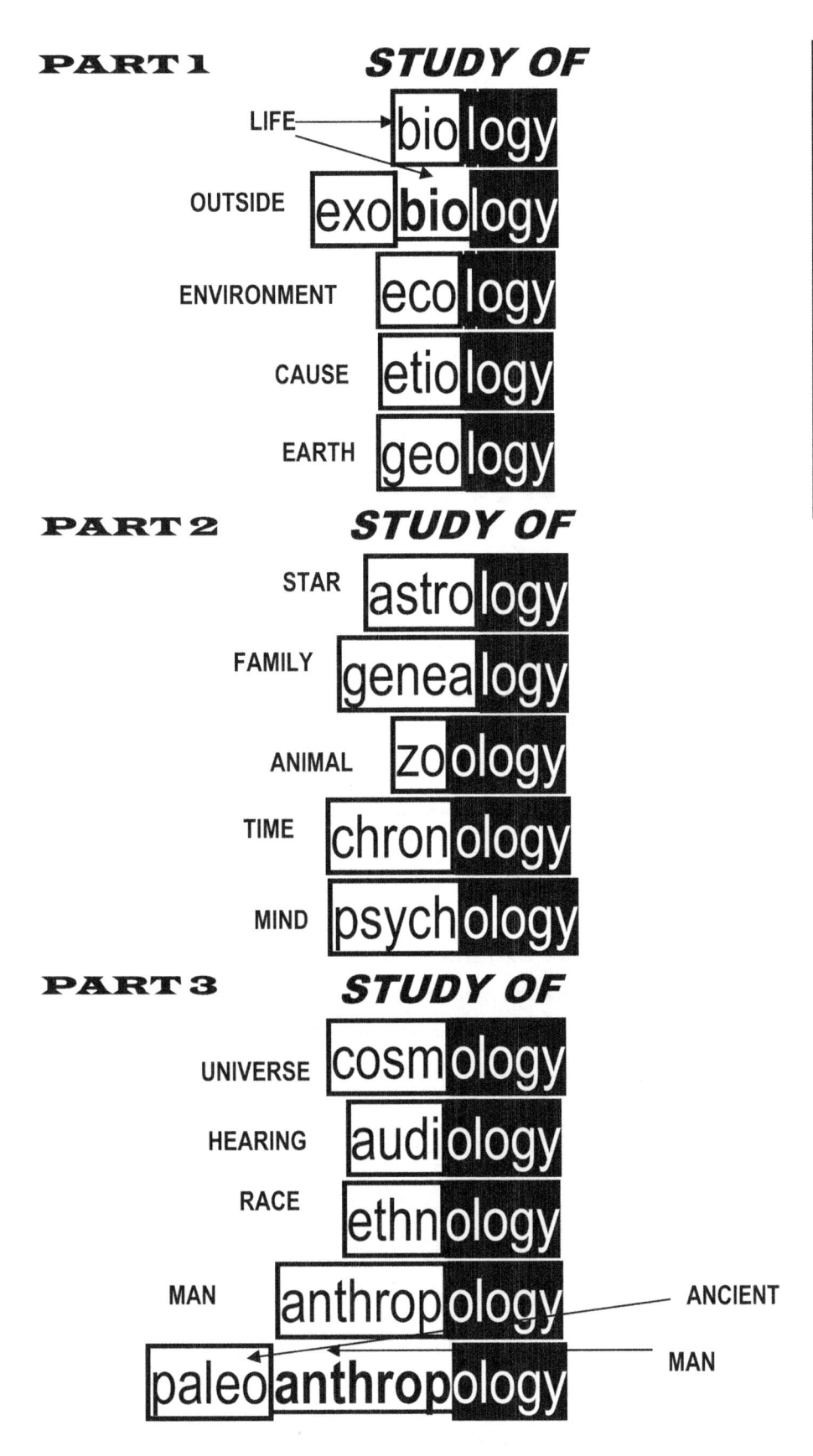

PART 2 — STUDY OF

- STAR — **astro**logy
- FAMILY — **genea**logy
- ANIMAL — **zo**ology
- TIME — **chron**ology
- MIND — **psych**ology

NOTEBOOK ACTIVITY

1. Write your own definition for each word.
2. Below your definition, write the Study Card Definition.

PART 3 — STUDY OF

- UNIVERSE — **cosm**ology
- HEARING — **audi**ology
- RACE — **ethn**ology
- MAN — **anthrop**ology
- ANCIENT / MAN — **paleo****anthrop**ology

Copyright 2020, Matthew Glavach, Ph.D.

STUDY CARD 1   **logy, ology–study of**   **GREEK**

biology (**bio- life**) the study of life and living organisms.

exobiology (**exo- outside, bio- life**) the search for and study of extraterrestrial living organisms.

ecology (**eco- environment**) the study of the interactions of organisms and their environment.

etiology (**etio- cause**) the study of causes, especially diseases.

geology (**geo- earth**) the study of the solid earth.

STUDY CARD 2   **logy, ology–study of**   **GREEK**

astrology (**astro- star**) the study that attempts to interpret the influence of the stars and heavenly bodies on human affairs.

genealogy (**genea- family**) the study of family histories; lineage.

zoology (**zo- animal**) the study of animals.

chronology (**chron- time**) the study related to measuring time and the ordering of events in time.

psychology (**psych- mind**) the study of the mind and its functions.

STUDY CARD 3   **logy, ology – study of**   **GREEK**

cosmology (**cosm- universe**) the study of the origin and development of the universe.

audiology (**audi- hearing**) the study of hearing disorders and their treatment.

ethnology (**ethn- race**) the study of different peoples (races) and their relationships.

anthropology (**anthrop- man**) the study of the origin, distribution, and development of man.

paleoanthropology (**paleo- ancient, anthrop- man**) the study of prehistoric man prior to homo sapiens.

Copyright 2020, Matthew Glavach, Ph.D.

Quiz 1 Latin and Greek Word Roots

Part 1. Write the word for the definition.

| biology | etiology | geology | exobiology | ecology |

1. _____ the study of the solid earth.
2. _____ the search for and study of extraterrestrial living organisms.
3. _____ the study of the interactions of organisms and their environment.
4. _____ the study of causes, especially diseases.
5. _____ the study of life and living organisms.

| astrology | genealogy | zoology | psychology | chronology |

6. _____ the study of family histories: lineage.
7. _____ the study of measuring time and the ordering of events in time.
8. _____ the study of animals.
9. _____ the study of the mind and its functions
10. _____ the study that attempts to interpret the influence of the stars and heavenly bodies on human affairs.

| audiology | anthropology | ethnology | cosmology | paleoanthropology |

11. _____ the study of different peoples (races) and their relationships.
12. _____ the study of hearing disorders and their treatment.
13. _____ the study of the origin and development of the universe.
14. _____ the study of the origin, distribution, and development of man.
15. _____ the study of prehistoric man prior to homo sapiens.

Part 2. Write the word root for each word.

| exo | geo | bio | eco | etio |

1. life_____ 2. cause_____ 3. earth_____ 4. outside_____ 5. environment_____

| genea | astro | zo | chron | psych |

6. star_____ 7. mind_____ 8. family_____ 9. time_____ 10. animal_____

| paleo | cosm | ethn | audi | anthrop |

11. universe_____ 12. race_____ 13. ancient_____ 14. man_____ 15. hearing_____

WORD CHART LESSON 2

biography
autobiography
bibliography
monograph
choreography

calligraphy
orthography
demography
geography
cartography

autograph
cryptography
chronograph
electrocardiograph
electroencephalograph

PART 1 — WRITTEN

- LIFE — **bio**graphy
- SELF → auto**bio**graphy ← LIFE
- BOOK — **biblio**graphy
- SINGLE — **mono**graph
- DANCE — **choreo**graphy

LESSON 2
graph/y
WRITING
WRITTEN
RECORDING

PART 2 — WRITING

- BEAUTIFUL — **calli**graphy
- CORRECT — **ortho**graphy
- PEOPLE — **demo**graphy
- EARTH — **geo**graphy
- MAP — **cart₍e₎o**graphy

PART 3 — WRITING, *RECORDING

- SELF — **auto**graph
- SECRET — **crypto**graphy
- TIME — *****chrono**graph
- ELECTRIC → *****electro**cardio**graph ← HEART
- *****electro**encephalo**graph ← BRAIN

NOTE:
A lesson part with two words at the top:
(WRITING, *RECORDING) an asterisk identifies which words go with word at the top.
*chronograph
*electrocardiograph
*electroencephalograph

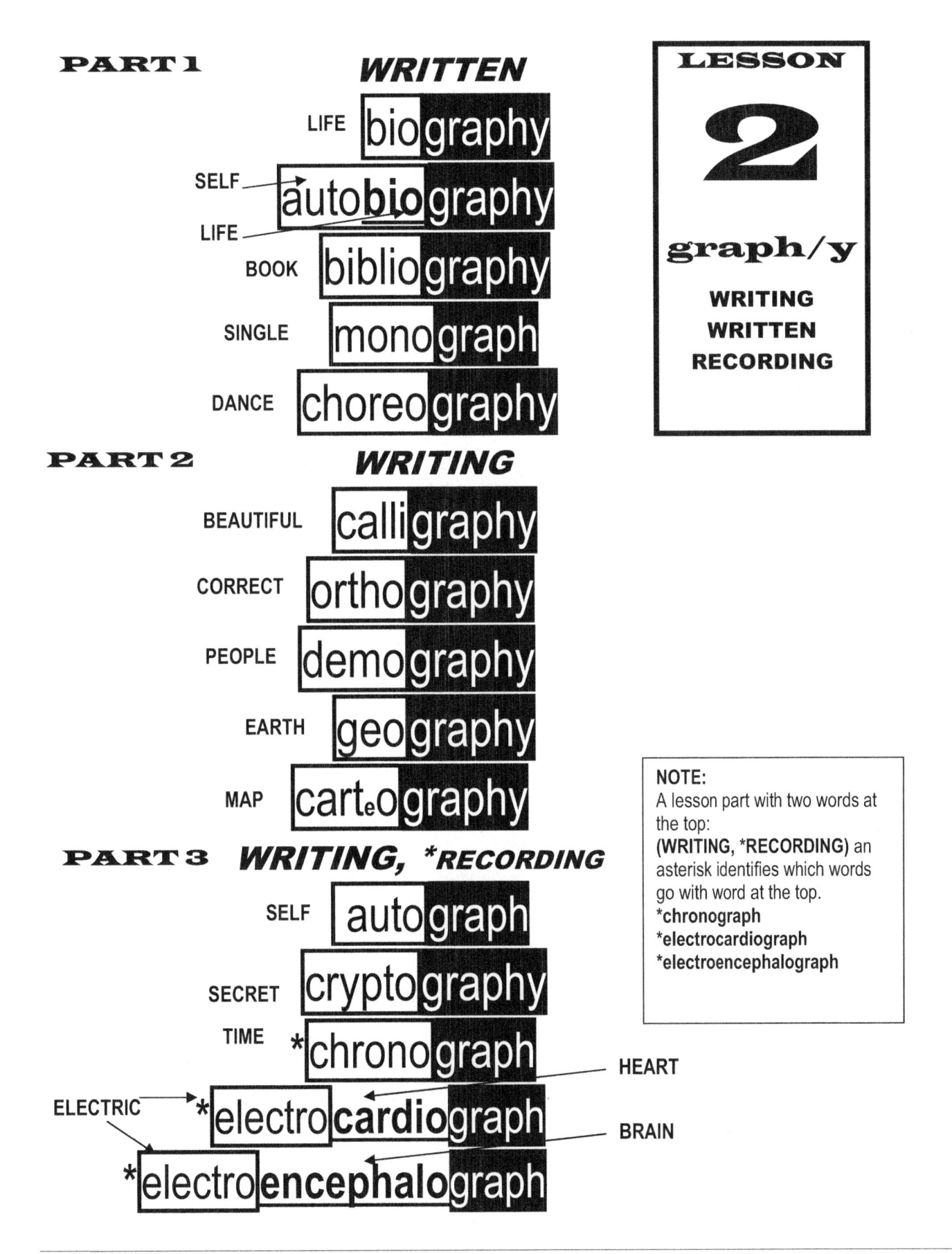

Copyright 2020, Matthew Glavach, Ph.D.

STUDY CARD 1   **graph, graphy – written**   **GREEK**

biography (**bio- life**) the story of one's life written by another.

autobiography (**auto- self, bio- life**) the story of one's life written by oneself.

bibliography (**biblio- book**) a list of books written on a specific subject. *A research paper always includes a bibliography.

monograph (**mono- single**) usually a scholarly article written on a single subject. *a long article or book on how the human body uses vitamin c.

choreography (**choreo- dance**) the written script for a dance sequence.

STUDY CARD 2   **graph, graphy – writing**   **GREEK**

calligraphy (**calli- beautiful**) the art of beautiful writing.

orthography (**ortho- correct**) correct spelling; the spelling system a language.

demography (**demo- people**) the study and writing about human populations as related to vital statistics, growth, etc.

geography (**geo- earth**) the science that does research, writes about, and makes maps of the earth.

cartography (**carto- map**) the art of map making.

STUDY CARD 3   **graph, graphy – writing, recording**   **GREEK**

autograph (**auto- self**) writing made by oneself, as in a signature.

cryptography (**crypto- secret**) the art of writing and deciphering (breaking) secret codes into normal language.

chronograph (**chrono- time**) an instrument for measuring (recording) brief time intervals; stopwatch.

electrocardiograph (**electro- electric; cardio- heart**) an instrument for graphically recording small electric currents in the heart.

electroencephalograph (**electro- electric; encephalo- brain**) an instrument for graphically recording small electric currents in the brain.

Quiz 2   Latin and Greek Word Roots

Part 1. Write the word for the definition

autobiography	choreography	monograph	bibliography	biography

1. _____ the story of one's life written by another.
2. _____ the story of one's life written by oneself.
3. _____ a list of books written on a specific subject.
4. _____ usually a scholarly article written on a single subject.
5. _____ the written script for a dance sequence.

demography	cartography	geography	calligraphy	orthography

6. _____ correct spelling; the spelling system of a language
7. _____ the art of beautiful writing.
8. _____ the science that does research, writes about, and makes maps of the earth.
9. _____ the art of map making.
10. _____ the study and writing about human populations as related to vital statistics,

electroencephalograph	chronograph	autograph	cryptography	electrocardiograph

11. _____ an instrument for measuring brief time intervals; stopwatch.
12. _____ writing made by one's own hand, as in a signature.
13. _____ the art of writing and deciphering (breaking) secret codes into normal language.
14. _____ an instrument for graphically recording small electric currents in the brain.
15. _____ an instrument for graphically recording small electric currents in the heart.

Part 2. Write the word root for each word.

crypto	ortho	bio	biblio	auto

1. life _____ 2. secret _____ 3. self _____ 4. correct _____ 5. book _____

carto	calli	geo	demo	choreo

6. earth _____ 7. map _____ 8. people _____ 9. dance _____ 10. beautiful _____

mono	chrono	encephalo	cardio	auto

11. self _____ 12. heart _____ 13. time _____ 14. single _____ 15. brain _____

elocution
evacuate
emigrate
emancipate
emissary

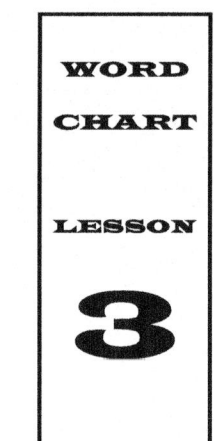

exclude
extol
extricate
exonerate
extemporaneous

extraordinary
extrapolate
extraneous
extraterrestrial
extrovert

WORD CHART LESSON 3

LESSON 3

e, ex

OUT

extra

OUTSIDE
BEYOND

PART 1 — OUT

- **e**locu**tion** — SPEAK
- **e**vacu**ate** — EMPTY
- **e**mig**rate** — MOVE
- **e**mancipate
- **e**miss**ary** — SEND

PART 2 — OUT

- ex**clude** — CLOSE
- ex**tol**
- ex**trica**te — HINDRANCES
- ex**onerate**
- ex**temporaneous**

PART 3 — BEYOND, *OUTSIDE

- **extra**ordinary
- **extra**polate
- **extra**neous
- **extra**ter**restrial** — EARTH
- *extro**vert** — TURN

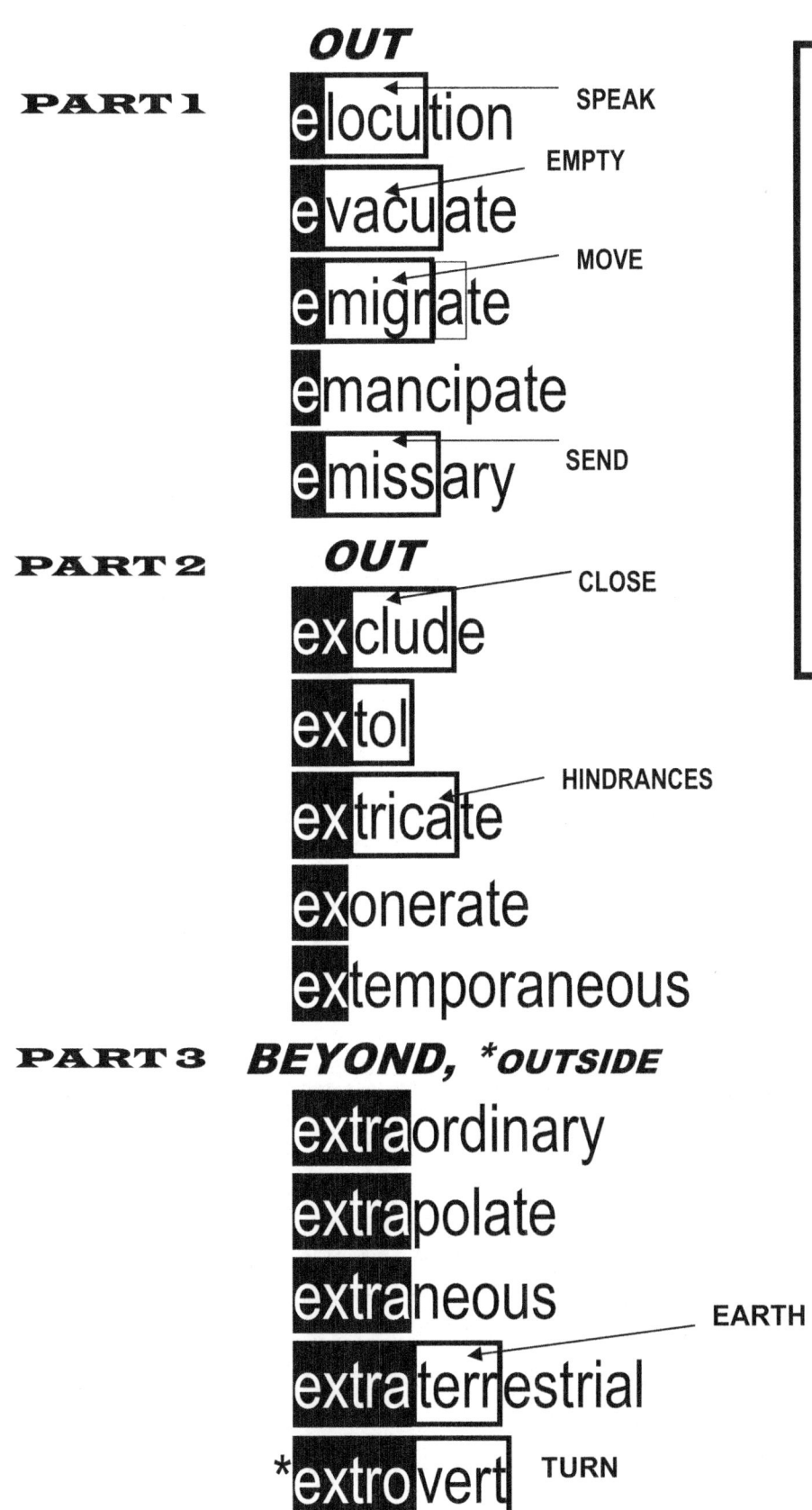

STUDY CARD 1 — e – out — LATIN

elocution (locu- to speak) to speak out; the art of public speaking or reading.

evacuate (vacu- empty) to empty out; to remove people from an area of danger.

emigrate (migr- move) to move out of a country or region to settle in another. *They emigrated from Russia to America.

emancipate - to take out of slavery or bondage; to liberate. *Abraham Lincoln emancipated the slaves; he set them free.

emissary (miss- send) a person sent out to represent a government, organization, or another person.

STUDY CARD 2 — ex - out — LATIN

exclude (clud- close) to close out; to not be included.

extol - to call out; to praise highly.

extricate (trica- hindrances) hindering; to take out or free someone from a difficult or dangerous situation. *Can you extricate yourself from your homework?

exonerate - to take out of guilt; to declare someone not guilty. *She was exonerated from the accusation of stealing.

extemporaneous – carried out with little or no preparation.

STUDY CARD 3 — extra – outside, beyond — LATIN

extraordinary - beyond ordinary.

extrapolate - go beyond or deduce (work out) from something that is known; to infer.

extraneous - extra, beyond what is needed; unnecessary.

extraterrestrial (terr- earth) occurring, existing, or originating outside of earth.

extrovert (vert- turn) outgoing; turning outward; an outgoing, overly expressive person. *Are you an extrovert or an introvert?

Quiz 3 — Latin and Greek Word Roots

Part 1. Write the word for the definition

| emigrate | emissary | emancipate | evacuate | elocution |

1. _____ to empty out; to remove people from an area of danger.
2. _____ a person sent out to represent a government, organization, or another person.
3. _____ to take out of slavery or bondage; to liberate.
4. _____ the art of public speaking or reading.
5. _____ to move out of a country or region to settle in another.

| extricate | exonerate | extol | extemporaneous | exclude |

6. _____ to call out; to praise highly.
7. _____ carried out with little or no preparation.
8. _____ hindering; to take out or free someone from a difficult or dangerous situation.
9. _____ to take out of guilt; to declare someone not guilty
10. _____ to close out; to not be included.

| extraordinary | extraneous | extraterrestrial | extrovert | extrapolate |

11. _____ outgoing; turning outward; an outgoing, overly expressive person.
12. _____ beyond ordinary.
13. _____ occurring, existing, or originating outside of earth.
14. _____ extra, beyond what is needed; unnecessary.
15. _____ go beyond or deduce (work out) from something that is known; to infer.

Part 2. Write the word root for each word.

| vert | terr | trica | clud | ex |

1. earth _____   2. turn _____   3. close _____   4. out _____   5. hindrances _____

| miss | e | migr | vacu | locu |

6. move _____   7. empty _____   8. send _____   9. out _____   10. to speak _____

17

Copyright 2020, Matthew Glavach, Ph.D.

WORD CHART LESSON 4

atheist
apathy
atrophy
amorphous
amnesia

anonymous
anorexia
anarchy
anemia
anesthesia

illiterate
immortal
incredulous
innocuous
irrevocable

LESSON 4

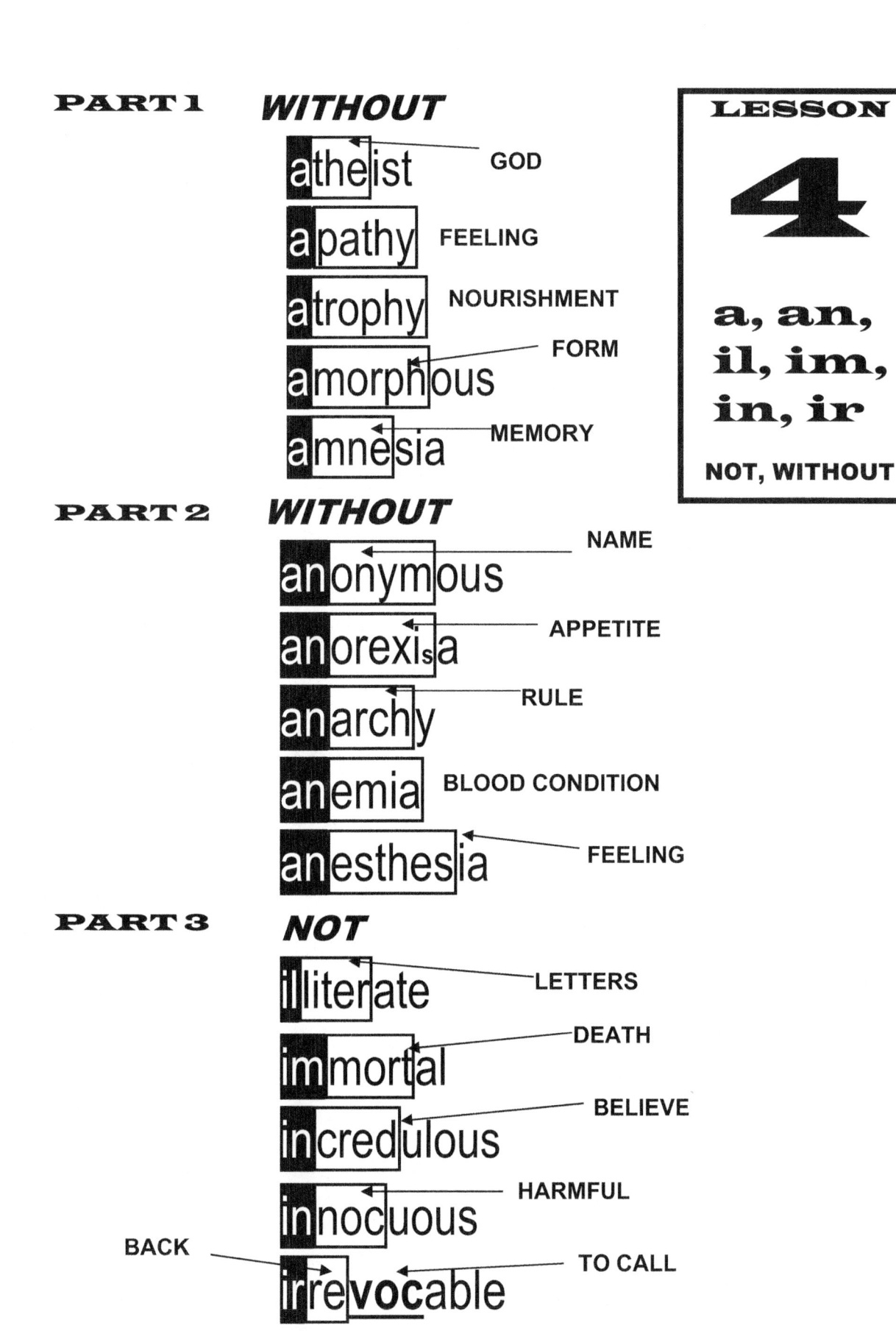

a, an, il, im, in, ir

NOT, WITHOUT

PART 1 — *WITHOUT*

- **a**theist — GOD
- **a**pathy — FEELING
- **a**trophy — NOURISHMENT
- **a**morphous — FORM
- **a**mnesia — MEMORY

PART 2 — *WITHOUT*

- **an**onymous — NAME
- **an**orexia — APPETITE
- **an**archy — RULE
- **an**emia — BLOOD CONDITION
- **an**esthesia — FEELING

PART 3 — *NOT*

- **il**literate — LETTERS
- **im**mortal — DEATH
- **in**credulous — BELIEVE
- **in**nocuous — HARMFUL
- **ir**re**voc**able — BACK / TO CALL

STUDY CARD 1   **a – without**   **GREEK**

atheist (the- God) without God; one who believes there is no God. *What is the difference between an atheist and an agnostic?

apathy (pathy- feeling) without feeling or emotion; indifference. *There is such voter apathy this year.

atrophy (trophy- nourishment)) a wasting away or failure to properly develop due to insufficient nourishment (nutrition).

amorphous (morp- form) without distinct shape or form; shapeless.

amnesia (mne- memory) without memory; a total or partial loss of memory due to injury etc. *His memory loss (amnesia) was due to dementia.

STUDY CARD 2   **an – without**   **GREEK**

anonymous (onym- name) 1. without a known name. 2. of unknown authorship or origin. *an anonymous tip.

anorexia (orexia- appetite) without a normal appetite; fear of gaining weight. *The actress later admitted she suffered from anorexia.

anarchy (arch- rule) without rule; lawlessness.

anemia (emia- blood condition) without enough healthy red blood cells to carry oxygen. *Anemia can cause fatigue and weakness.

anesthesia (esthes- feeling) without feeling. *He received anesthesia before surgery to block the feeling of pain.

STUDY CARD 3   **il, im, in, ir – not**   **LATIN**

illiterate (liter- letters) 1. not able to read and write. 2. displaying a lack of culture, especially in literature and language.

immortal (mort- death) 1. not subject to death. 2. having everlasting fame. *The "Immortals" of the rugby league in Australia are the greatest ever.

incredulous (cred- believe) not believing; skeptical. *The teacher looked incredulous after hearing the student's excuse for being tardy.

innocuous (noc- harmful) not harmful; uninspiring. *an innocuous speech.

irrevocable (re- back; voc- to call) not able to be called back or undone; final. *She thought the financing arrangement was irrevocable.

Quiz 4 Latin and Greek Word Roots

Part 1. Write the word for the definition.

| atheist | amorphous | atrophy | amnesia | apathy |

1. _____ without distinct shape or form; shapeless.
2. _____ without feeling or emotion; indifference.
3. _____ without God; one who believes there is no God.
4. _____ without memory; a total or partial loss of memory due to injury etc.
5. _____ a wasting away or failure to properly develop due to insufficient nourishment (nutrition).

| anesthesia | anemia | anorexia | anonymous | anarchy |

6. _____ [1.] without a known name. [2.] of unknown authorship or origin.
7. _____ without rule; lawlessness.
8. _____ without a normal appetite; fear of gaining weight.
9. _____ without feeling.
10. _____ without enough healthy red blood cells to carry oxygen.

| innocuous | irrevocable | incredulous | illiterate | immortal |

11. _____ [1.] not subject to death. [2.] having everlasting fame.
12. _____ not believing; skeptical.
13. _____ not harmful; uninspiring.
14. _____ not able to be called back or undone; final.
15. _____ [1.] not able to read and write. [2.] displaying a lack of culture, especially in literature and language.

Part 2. Write the word root for each word.

| the | onym | pathy | trophy | mne |

1. feeling _____ 2. memory _____ 3. name _____ 4. God _____ 5. nourishment _____

| orexia | emia | esthes | liter | mort |

6. death _____ 7. letters _____ 8. feeling _____ 9. blood _____ 10. appetite _____

| cred | re | liter | voc | noc |

11. back _____ 12. call _____ 13. harmful _____ 14. believe _____ 15. letters _____

WORD CHART LESSON 5

precaution
premonition
precursor
predecessor
precocious

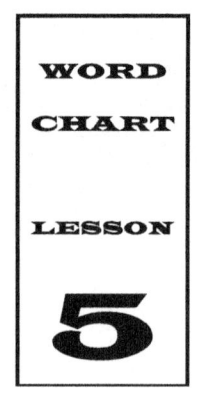

prognosis
prologue
im**pro**vise
provident
procrastinate

postnatal
posthumous
postlude
posterior
posterity

LESSON 5

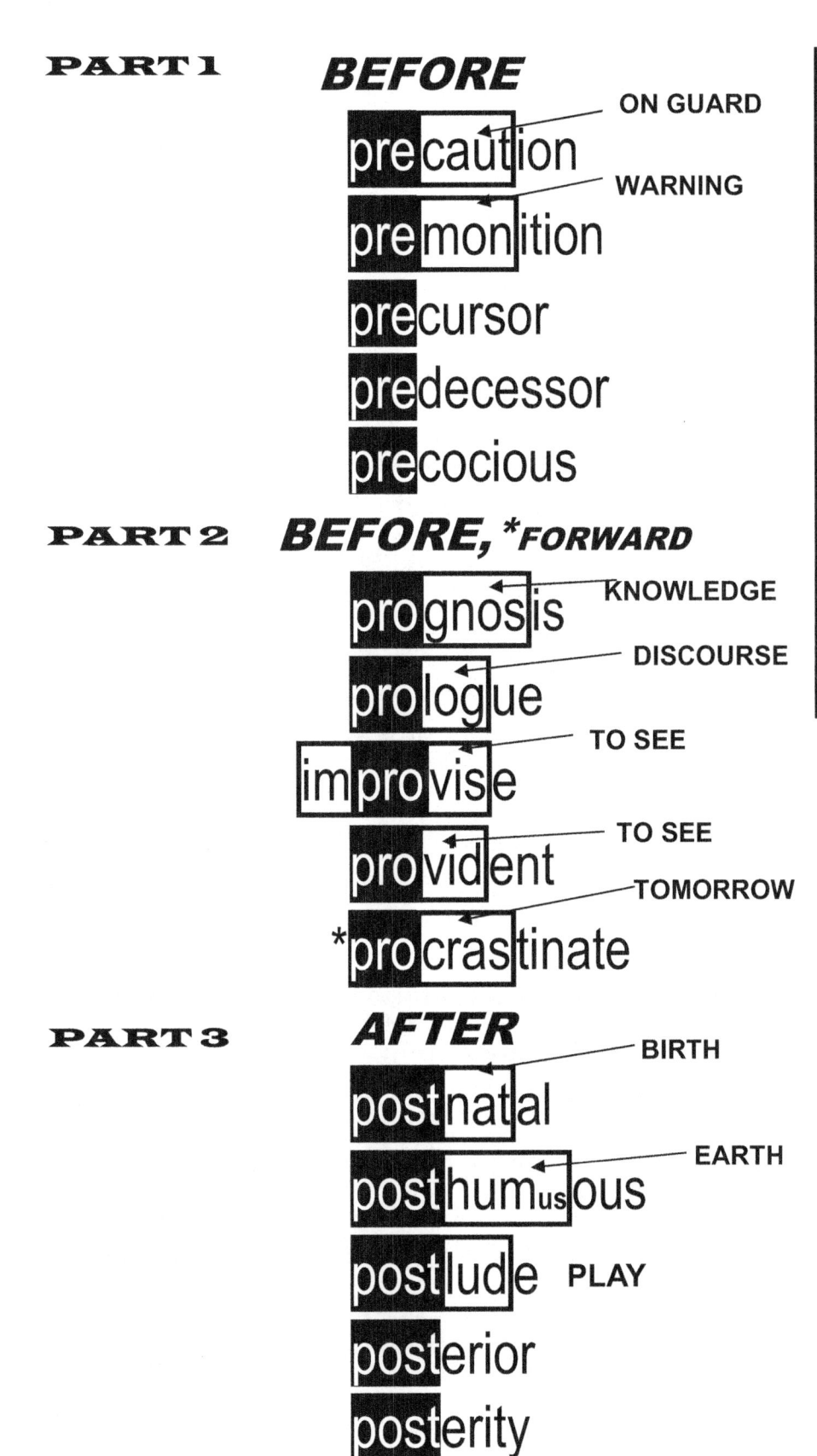

pre — BEFORE
pro — BEFORE, FORWARD
post — AFTER

PART 1 — *BEFORE*

- pre|caution — ON GUARD
- pre|monition — WARNING
- precursor
- predecessor
- precocious

PART 2 — *BEFORE, *FORWARD*

- pro|gnosis — KNOWLEDGE
- pro|logue — DISCOURSE
- im|pro|vise — TO SEE
- pro|vident — TO SEE
- *pro|crastinate — TOMORROW

PART 3 — *AFTER*

- post|natal — BIRTH
- post|hum(us)|ous — EARTH
- post|lude — PLAY
- posterior
- posterity

STUDY CARD 1 — pre - before (LATIN)

precaution (caut- on guard) cautious, being on guard beforehand.

premonition (mon- warn) an intense feeling, often warning of danger to come. *She had a premonition about a plane crash, so she took the train.

precursor - a thing that comes before and indicates the approach of another thing; forerunner. *Is sneezing a precursor to a cold?

predecessor - someone or something that came before.

precocious - a child who develops before others. *What a precocious child; reading novels before the age of four.

STUDY CARD 2 — pro – before, forward (GREEK)

prognosis (gnos- knowledge) to know before; the likely course of a disease or ailment. *The disease has a poor prognosis.

prologue (log- discourse) an introduction before a discourse, poem, or play. *Before the play began, the narrator read the prologue to the play.

im**pro**vise (im- not; vis- see) to see before; to compose, sing, or recite without preparation. *Without prior notice; she had to improvise much of her speech.

provident (vid- see) to see before; to prepare for the future; prudent. *His past money problems made him more careful and provident.

procrastinate (cras- tomorrow) to move forward; to put off until tomorrow, or a later time, something that could be done today.

STUDY CARD 3 — post - after (LATIN)

postnatal (nat- birth) existing or happening after birth.

posthumous (humus- earth) occurring and continuing after a person's death. *She was awarded the medal of honor posthumously.

postlude (lud- play) to play after; a concluding piece of music, especially an organ at the end of a church service.

posterior - located at or near the back. *In anatomy class, we learned that "posterior" refers to the back of a body.

posterity - all who come after; the future generations of a family. *An example of posterity is grandchildren.

Copyright 2020, Matthew Glavach, Ph.D.

Quiz 5 — Latin and Greek Word Roots

Part 1. Write the word for the definition.

| precursor | precaution | premonition | predecessor | precocious |

1. _____ an intense feeling, often warning of danger to come
2. _____ a thing that comes before and indicates the approach of another thing; forerunner.
3. _____ cautious, being on guard beforehand.
4. _____ a child who develops before others.
5. _____ someone or something that came before.

| procrastinate | prologue | improvise | prognosis | provident |

6. _____ to know before; the likely course of a disease or ailment.
7. _____ an introduction before a discourse, poem, or play.
8. _____ to see before; to compose, sing, or recite without preparation.
9. _____ to see before; to prepare for the future; prudent.
10. _____ to move forward; to put off until tomorrow, or a later time, something that could be done today.

| posterity | posterior | posthumous | postnatal | postlude |

11. _____ existing or happening after birth.
12. _____ all who come after; the future generations of a family.
13. _____ located at or near the back.
14. _____ occurring and continuing after a person's death
15. _____ to play after; a concluding piece of music, especially an organ at the end of a church service.

Part 2. Write the word root for each word.

| mon | pre | gnos | log | caut |

1. discourse _____ 2. on guard _____ 3. before _____ 4. warn _____ 5. knowledge _____

| lud | humus | nat | cras | vid, vis |

6. earth _____ 7. birth _____ 8. see _____ 9. play _____ 10. tomorrow _____

descend
debilitate
degenerate
decelerate
debacle

subjugate
subversive
subliminal
subordinate
subterranean

supervisor
supercilious
superlative
superfluous
superstition

WORD CHART LESSON 6

PART 1 — ***DOWN***

- **de**scend — CLIMB
- **de**bilitate
- **de**generate
- **de**celerate — SPEED
- **de**bacle

PART 2 — ***UNDER***

- **sub**jugate
- **sub**versive — TURN
- **sub**liminal
- **sub**ordinate — CONTROL
- **sub**terranean — EARTH, LAND

PART 3 — ***ABOVE, *BEYOND***

- **super**visor — SEE, LOOK
- **super**cilious
- *****super**lative
- *****super**fluous — FLOW
- *****super**stition

LESSON 6

de — DOWN, AWAY

sub — UNDER, BELOW, DOWN

super — ABOVE, BEYOND

STUDY CARD 1 — de – down — LATIN

descend (scend- climb) to climb down.

debilitate – to break down; to weaken.

degenerate - to break down; to deteriorate. *Her old neighborhood had degenerated into a terrible slum.

decelerate (celer- quickness, speed) to slow down; opposite of accelerate. *He ran his truck off the road because there was no time to decelerate.

debacle - a sudden breakdown; a complete failure. *What was the greatest financial debacle in United States history?

STUDY CARD 2 — sub – under, below — LATIN

subjugate - to bring under domination or control, especially by conquest. *They did not seek to destroy, only subjugate the small country.

subversive (vers- turn) to turn on; to undermine. *Their subversive behavior undermines the country's authority.

subliminal - under the threshold of sensation or consciousness; subconscious *affecting someone's mind without their being aware of it.

subordinate (ord- control) a person under influence or control of another person; as in a job or the military.

subterranean (terr- earth) under the earth; below the ground.

STUDY CARD 3 — super – above, beyond — LATIN

supervisor (vis- to look) one who is above; looks over the work of others.

supercilious - above, acting superior or pompous. *The supercilious lady always boasted about her castles and sports cars.

superlative - to go beyond; highest quality; best.

superfluous (flu- flow) overflowing; beyond what is needed; unnecessary. *Any further discussion of this paper would be superfluous.

superstition - beyond reason or scientific knowledge; "Friday the 13th"; "breaking a mirror". *Do you have a superstition?

Copyright 2020, Matthew Glavach, Ph.D.

Quiz 6 — Latin and Greek Word Roots

Part 1. Write the word for the definition.

| debacle | degenerate | decelerate | debilitate | descend |

1. _____ to break down; to deteriorate.
2. _____ to climb down.
3. _____ to slow down; opposite of accelerate.
4. _____ a sudden breakdown; a complete failure.
5. _____ to break down; to weaken

| subjugate | subliminal | subordinate | subterranean | subversive |

6. _____ under the earth; below the ground.
7. _____ to turn on; to undermine.
8. _____ under the threshold of sensation or consciousness.
9. _____ to bring under domination or control, especially by conquest.
10. _____ a person under the influence or control of another person; as in a job or the military.

| supervisor | supercilious | superstition | superfluous | superlative |

11. _____ one who is above; looks over the work of others.
12. _____ to go beyond; highest quality; best.
13. _____ overflowing; beyond what is needed; unnecessary.
14. _____ above, acting superior or pompous.
15. _____ beyond reason or scientific knowledge

Part 2. Write the word root for each word.

| scend | celer | vers | ord | terr |

1. climb _____ 2. turn _____ 3. control _____ 4. earth _____ 5. speed _____

| vis | super | flu | de | sub |

6. below _____ 7. look _____ 8. flow _____ 9. above _____ 10. down, away _____

WORD CHART LESSON 7

ex**ceed**
pre**cede**
re**cede**
inter**cede**
con**cede**

con**duct**
ductile
aque**duct**
se**duce**
in**duct**

con**clude**
pre**clude**
se**clude**
ex**clus**ive
incon**clus**ive

LESSON 7

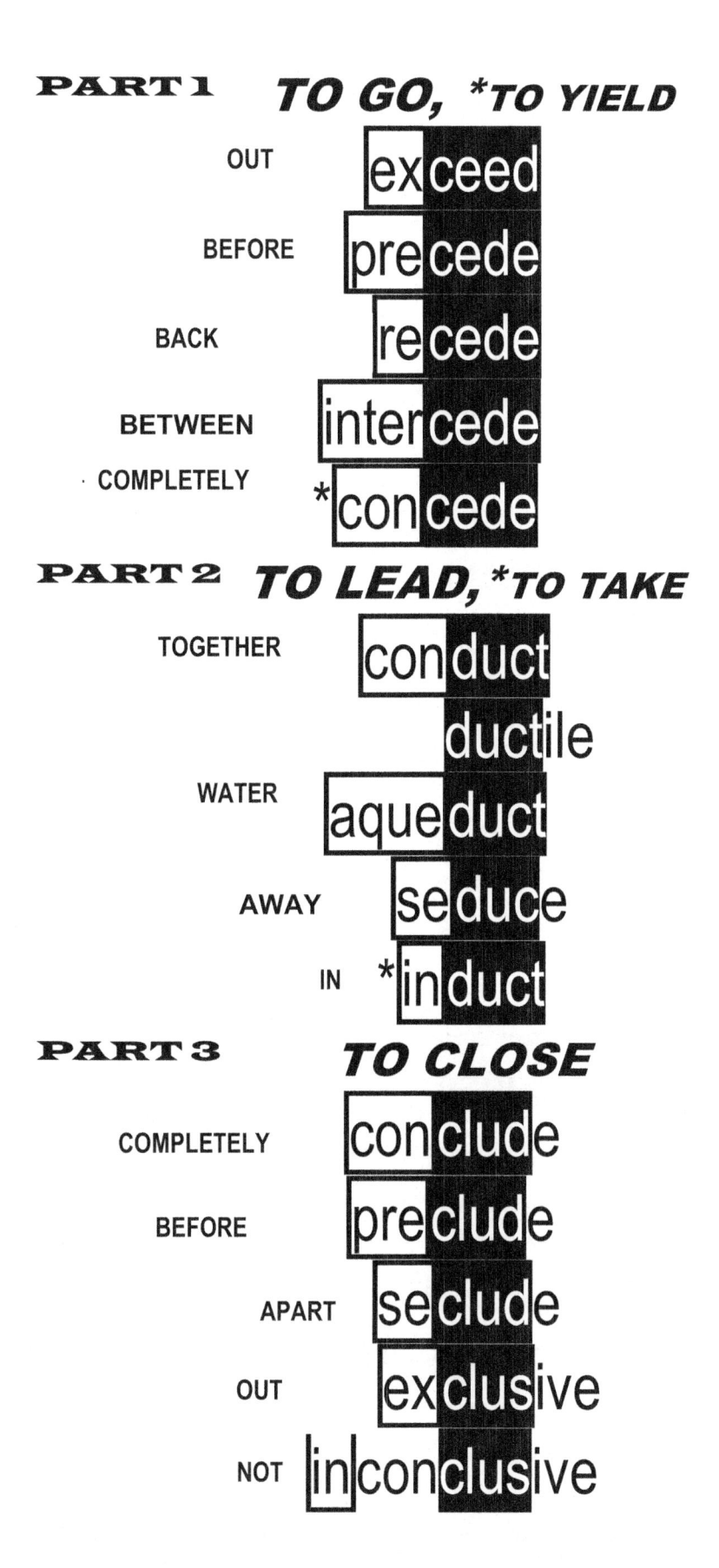

ceed
cede
TO GO, TO YIELD

duct
TO LEAD, TO TAKE

clud
clus
TO CLOSE

PART 1 — *TO GO, *TO YIELD*

- OUT — **ex**ceed
- BEFORE — **pre**cede
- BACK — **re**cede
- BETWEEN — **inter**cede
- COMPLETELY — *****con**cede

PART 2 — *TO LEAD, *TO TAKE*

- TOGETHER — **con**duct
- ductile
- WATER — **aque**duct
- AWAY — **se**duce
- IN — ***in**duct

PART 3 — *TO CLOSE*

- COMPLETELY — **con**clude
- BEFORE — **pre**clude
- APART — **se**clude
- OUT — **ex**clusive
- NOT — **in**conclusive

STUDY CARD 1 — **ceed, cede – to go, to yield** — LATIN

exceed (ex- out) to go outside or beyond a set limit; speeding, etc.

precede (pre- before) to go before.

recede (re- back) to go back or move away; withdraw. *The flood waters finally began to recede.

intercede (inter- between) to go between; to mediate. *The lawyer will intercede for his client.

concede (con- completely) to surrender or yield. *The warden would not concede to the prisoners' demands.

STUDY CARD 2 — **duc/t – to lead, to take** — LATIN

conduct (con- together) to act as a leader of or director of (usually a group). *to conduct a class. * to conduct an orchestra.

ductile - easily led or persuaded; gullible.

aqueduct (aqu- water) a large channel or pipe used to take water from a remote supply.

seduce (se- away) to lead away; lure; or entice from proper conduct.

induct (in- into) to take into; to be inducted into the armed forces.

STUDY CARD 3 — **clud, clus - close** — LATIN

conclude (con- completely) to close completely; to bring an end to; finish.

preclude (pre- before) to close off; to prevent before ever happening. *She feared her finances would preclude her from attending college.

seclude (se- apart) to be closed off from, apart from social contact.

exclusive (ex- out) closed out except for one thing; limiting or limited to use by a single individual or group. *an exclusive interview.

inconclusive (in- not) not leading to a result or outcome. *The results from the survey were inconclusive.

Copyright 2020, Matthew Glavach, Ph.D.

Quiz 7 — Latin and Greek Word Roots

Part 1. Write the word for the definition.

| exceed | intercede | concede | recede | precede |

1. _____ to go before.
2. _____ to go outside or beyond a set limit; speeding, etc.
3. _____ to go back or move away; withdraw.
4. _____ to go between; to mediate.
5. _____ to surrender or yield

| seduce | ductile | induct | conduct | aqueduct |

6. _____ easily led or persuaded; gullible.
7. _____ to lead away; lure; or entice from proper conduct.
8. _____ to act as a leader of or director of (usually a group)
9. _____ to take into; to be inducted into the armed forces.
10. _____ a large channel or pipe used to take water from a remote supply.

| inconclusive | exclusive | preclude | conclude | seclude |

11. _____ to close completely; to bring an end to; finish.
12. _____ to be closed off from, apart from social contact.
13. _____ to close off; to prevent before ever happening.
14. _____ not leading to a result or outcome.
15. _____ closed out except for one thing; limiting or limited to use by a single individual or group.

Part 2. Write the word root for each word.

| ex | pre | re | inter |

1. before _____ 2. between _____ 3. out _____ 4. back _____

| aqu | se | con | con |

5. away _____ 6. water _____ 7. together _____ 8. completely _____

| cede | duct | clud, clus | in |

9. not _____ 10. close _____ 11. lead, take _____ 12. to go; to yield _____

diameter
dialogue
diagnosis
dialectic
diaphanous

transfer
transport
transition
transgress
transparent

transcend
transient
translucent
in**trans**igent
transaction

WORD CHART LESSON 8

LESSON 8

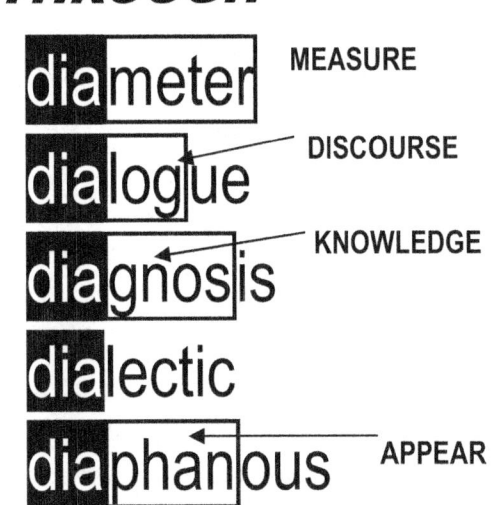

dia — THROUGH, ACROSS
trans — THROUGH

PART 1 — *THROUGH*

- **dia**meter — MEASURE
- **dia**logue — DISCOURSE
- **dia**gnosis — KNOWLEDGE
- **dia**lectic
- **dia**phanous — APPEAR

PART 2 — *ACROSS, *THROUGH*

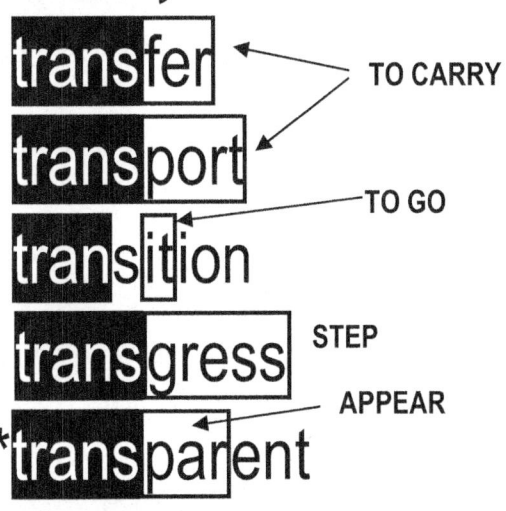

- **trans**fer — TO CARRY
- **trans**port — TO CARRY
- **trans**ition — TO GO
- **trans**gress — STEP
- *****trans**parent — APPEAR

PART 3 — *THROUGH, *BEYOND*

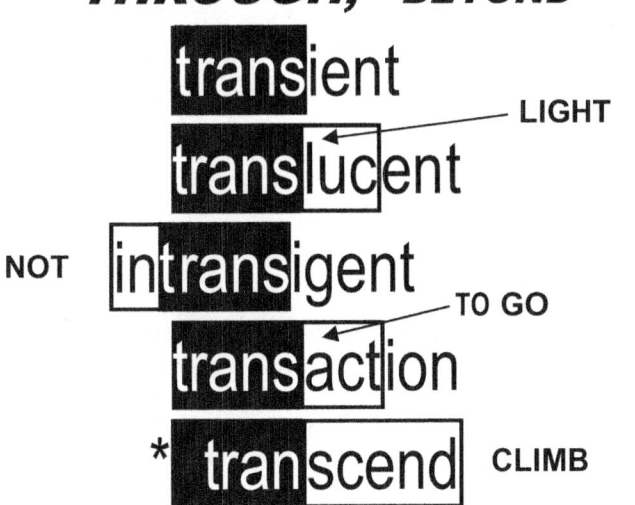

- **trans**ient
- **trans**lucent — LIGHT
- in**trans**igent — NOT
- **trans**action — TO GO
- *****trans**cend — CLIMB

STUDY CARD 1   **dia – through**   GREEK

diameter **(meter- measure)** a straight line that measures the distance through the center of a circle.

dialogue **(log- discourse)** through discourse; written and spoken communication *a discussion between two or more people. *the dialogue between two people as in a play.

diagnosis **(gnos- knowledge)** to know through knowledge. *to diagnose a disease through its signs and symptoms.

dialectic - to establish a truth through a reasoned argument. *a logical discourse between two or more people having different points of view.

diaphanous **(phan- to appear)** a fabric that appears so sheer as to be seen through. *She was shocked when she put on her dress made of a diaphanous fabric.

STUDY CARD 2   **trans – through, across**   LATIN

transfer **(fer- to carry)** to carry across; to move from one place to another. *a transfer to a new job.

transport **(port- to carry)** to carry across; to carry, move, or convey people or goods, especially over long distances.

transition **(it- to go)** moving across; the process of going from one state or condition to another. * in transition from one job to another.

transgress **(gress- step)** to step across the line between good and evil.

transparent **(par- appear)** to allow light to pass through so that objects appear clear and distinguished.

STUDY CARD 3   **trans – through, beyond**   LATIN

transcend **(scend- climb)** to climb beyond or above; to surpass. *Her basketball skills transcend most players.

transient - passing through; one who is not staying a long time. *guests in a hotel.

translucent **(luc- light)** allowing light to pass through but objects are not clearly distinguished; semitransparent.

in**trans**igent **(in- not)** not willing to compromise; unyielding. *Her mother had tried persuasion, but she was intransigent.

transaction **(act- to drive)** to drive through, to conduct or negotiate, especially in business affairs.

Quiz 8 — Latin and Greek Word Roots

Part 1. Write the word for the definition.

diaphanous	diagnosis	dialogue	diameter	dialectic

1. _____ through discourse; written and spoken communication.
2. _____ to know through knowledge.
3. _____ to establish a truth through a reasoned argument.
4. _____ a fabric that appears so sheer as to be seen through.
5. _____ a straight line that <u>measures</u> the distance <u>through</u> the center of a circle.

transgress	transition	transfer	transport	transparent

6. _____ moving across; the process of going from one state or condition to another.
7. _____ to carry across; to move from one place to another.
8. _____ to step across the line between good and evil.
9. _____ to allow light to pass through so that objects appear clear and distinguished.
10. _____ to carry across; to carry, move, or convey people or goods, especially over long distances.

transaction	translucent	transcend	transient	intransigent

11. _____ passing through; one who is not staying a long time.
12. _____ not willing to compromise; unyielding
13. _____ to drive through, to conduct or negotiate, especially in business affairs.
14. _____ to climb beyond or above; to surpass.
15. _____ allowing light to pass through but objects are not clearly distinguished; semitransparent.

Part 2. Write the word root for each word.

meter	log	gnos	phan

1. appear _____   2. knowledge _____   3. discourse _____   4. measure _____

port	act	gress	par

5. carry _____   6. drive _____   7. step _____   8. appear _____

scend	luc	in	trans

9. not _____   10. through _____   11. light _____   12. climb _____

WORD CHART LESSON 9

synchronize
a**syn**chronous
synthesis
syllable
idio**syn**crasy

sympathy
syntax
symphony
symbiosis
symposium

coalesce
collaborate
collusion
confluence
congregate

LESSON 9

syn
sym
SAME
TOGETHER

co
con
WITH
TOGETHER

PART 1 — TOGETHER

- **syn**chron**ize** — TIME
- NOT a**syn**chron**ous** — TIME
- **syn**the**sis** — TO PUT
- **syl**lab**le** — GATHER, TAKE
- PECULIAR idio**syn**crasy

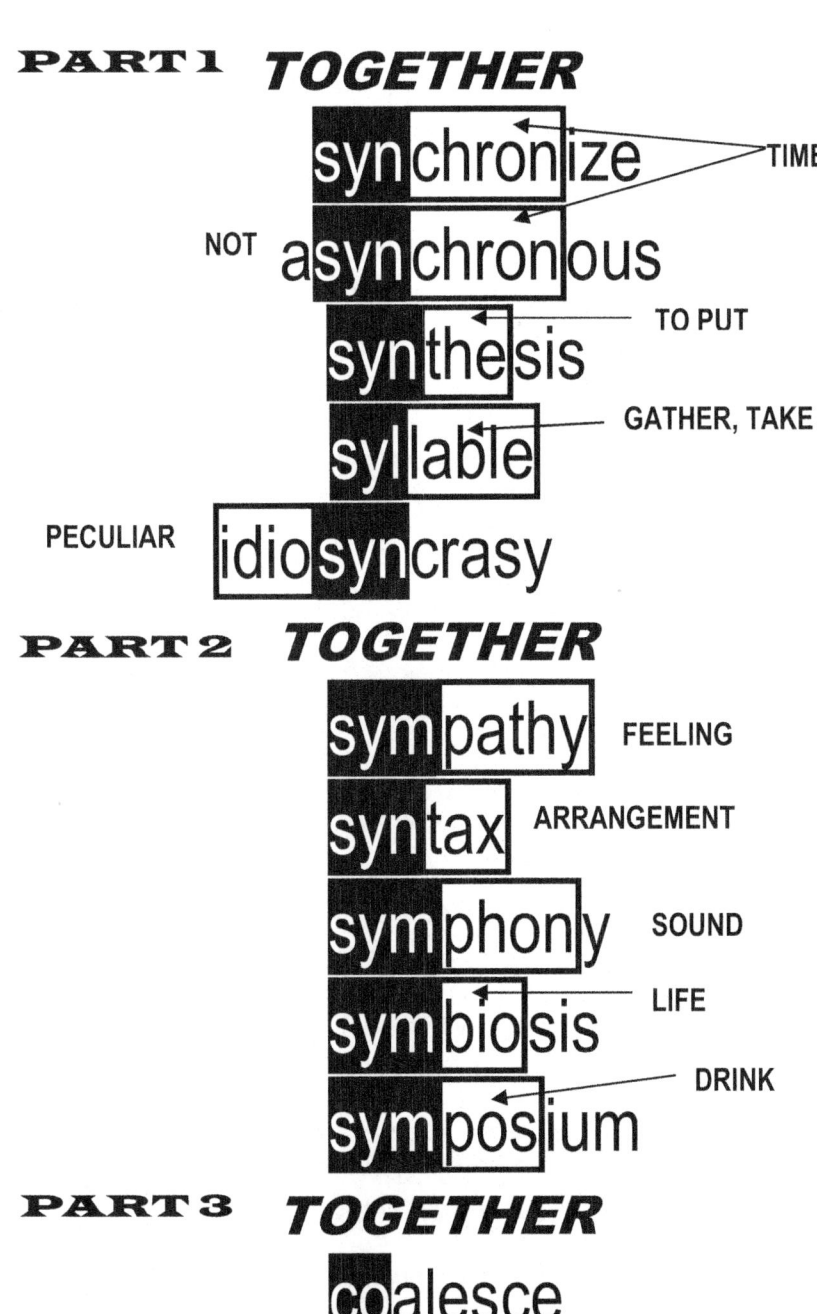

PART 2 — TOGETHER

- **sym**pathy — FEELING
- **syn**tax — ARRANGEMENT
- **sym**phony — SOUND
- **sym**bio**sis** — LIFE
- **sym**pos**ium** — DRINK

PART 3 — TOGETHER

- **co**alesce
- **col**laborate
- **col**lusion
- **con**flu**ence** — FLOW
- **con**greg**ate** — FLOCK

STUDY CARD 1   **syn, syl – together**   GREEK

synchronize (chron- time) to cause to occur together; at the same time.

a**syn**chronous (a- not; chron- time) not occurring (together) at the same time.

synthesis (the- put) putting things together into a meaningful whole.

syllable (lable- gather, take) letters gathered together to form a single uninterrupted sound. *Ball* has one sound/syllable. *Basketball* has 3 syllables.

idio**syn**crasy (ideo- peculiar) a physical or mental characteristic peculiar to a person.

STUDY CARD 2   **syn, sym - together**   GREEK

sympathy (pathy- feeling) sharing feelings together; sharing and understanding, another person's feelings: sorrow, trouble, etc.

syntax (tax- arrangement) the arrangement of words and phrases together; to create well-formed sentences in a language.

symphony (phon- sounds) a harmony of sounds and colors; a concert by a symphony orchestra.

symbiosis (bio- living) two dissimilar species living together for mutual benefit of each; mutually beneficial relationships between persons, etc.

symposium (pos- to drink) a coming together for intellectual discussion and drinks. In ancient Greece - a symposium was a drinking party with intellectual discussion.

STUDY CARD 3   **co, con, com – with, together**   LATIN

coalesce - to come together as one; to unite. The Southern coalition in Congress often vote the same way.

collaborate - work together on an activity, especially to produce or create something.

collusion - secret or illegal cooperation (together) or conspiracy, especially in order to cheat or deceive others.

confluence (flu- flow) a flowing together, especially, of rivers, and where they begin to flow together. *the confluence of the Laramie and North Platte Rivers.

congregate (greg- flock) to come (flock) together. *Most of the congregation attended the service.

Quiz 9 — Latin and Greek Word Roots

Part 1. Write the word for the definition.

synchronize   synthesis   asynchronous   syllable   idiosyncrasy

1. _____ putting things together into a meaningful whole.
2. _____ not occurring together at the same time.
3. _____ to cause to occur together; at the same time.
4. _____ a physical or mental characteristic peculiar to a person.
5. _____ letters gathered-together to form a single uninterrupted sound.

symposium   syntax   sympathy   symphony   symbiosis

6. _____ a harmony of sounds and colors
7. _____ two dissimilar species living together for mutual benefit of each
8. _____ sharing feelings together
9. _____ a coming together for intellectual discussion and drinks.
10. _____ the arrangement of words and phrases together; to create well-formed sentences in a language.

collusion   congregate   coalesce   confluence   collaborate

11. _____ work together on an activity, especially to produce or create something.
12. _____ to come together as one; to unite. (often vote the same way.)
13. _____ secret or illegal cooperation or conspiracy.
14. _____ to come (flock) together. *Most of the congregation attended the service".
15. _____ a flowing together, especially, of rivers, and where they begin to flow together.

Part 2. Write the word root for each word.

onym   the   lable   chron

1. name _____   2. time _____   3. put _____   4. gather, take _____

ideo   pathy   tax   phon

5. sounds _____   6. peculiar _____   7. feeling _____   8. arrangement _____

bio   pos   flu   greg

9. flock _____   10. flow _____   11. to drink _____   12. living _____

WORD CHART LESSON 10

intro**spec**tion
per**spec**tive
speculation
circum**spec**t
specter

visible
vista
visionary
pro**vid**ent
e**vid**ent

tele**scop**e
horo**scop**e
con**spic**uous
au**spic**ious
per**spic**acious

LESSON 10

spec — LOOK, SEE
vis, vid
scop — SEE, VIEW

PART 1 — *LOOK, SEE*

- INTO — **intro**spection
- THROUGH — **per**spective
- speculation
- AROUND — **circum**spect
- specter

PART 2 — *SEE*

- **vis**ible — ABLE TO
- vista
- visionary
- BEFORE — **pro**vident
- OUT — **e**vident

PART 3 — *SEE*

- DISTANT — **tele**scope
- HOUR — **horo**scope
- COMPLETELY — **con**spicuous
- **au**spicious
- THROUGH — **per**spicacious

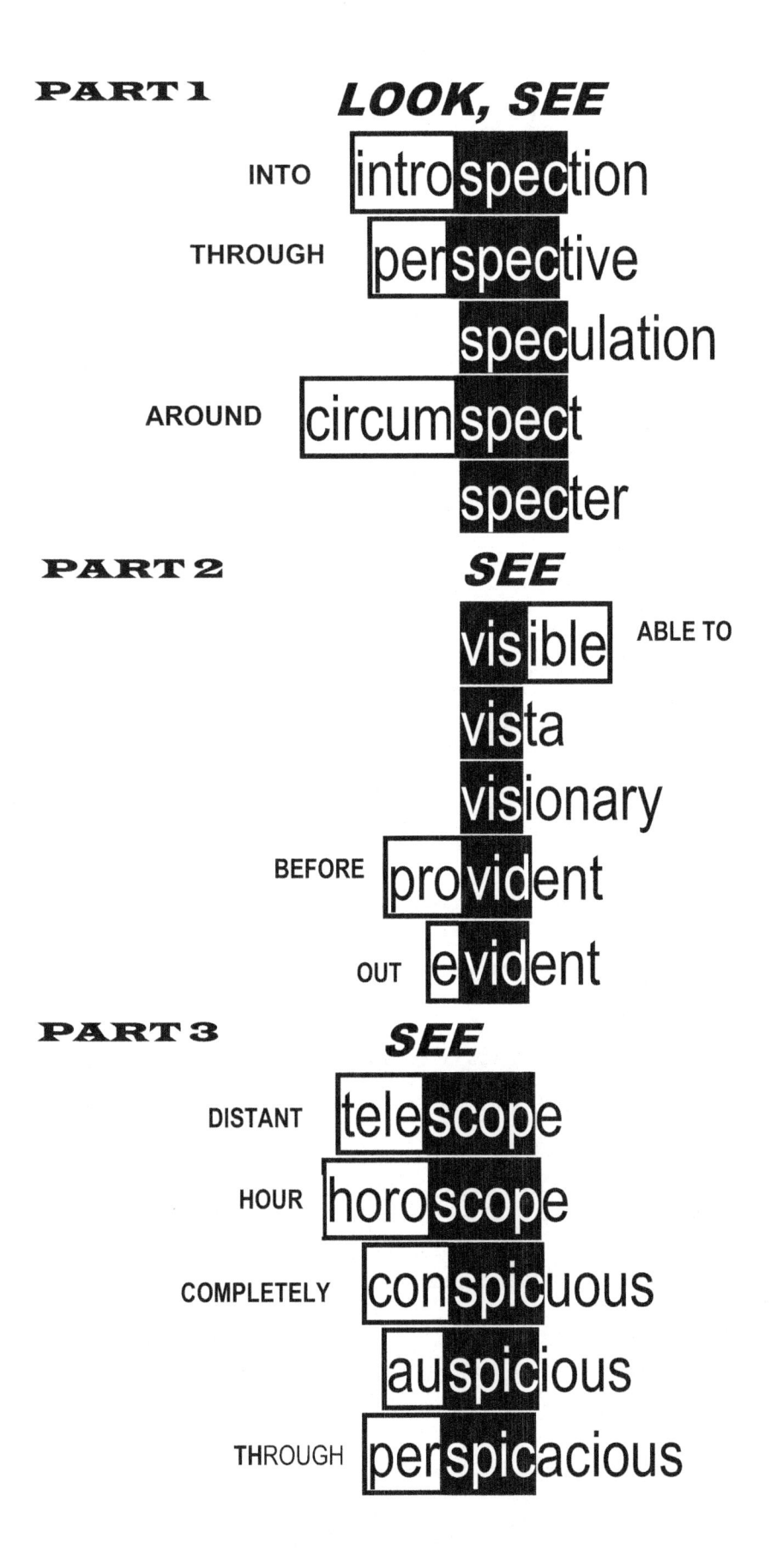

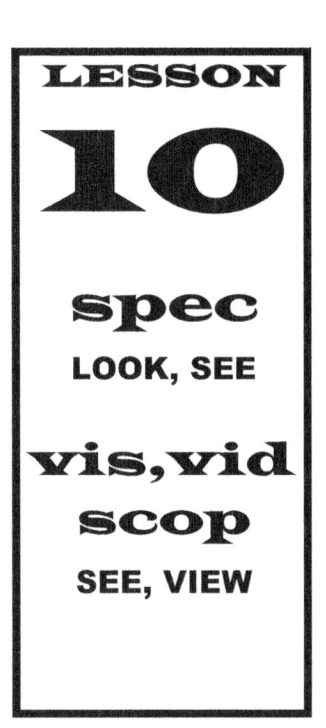

STUDY CARD 1 — spec – look, see — LATIN

introspec**tion (intro- into)** self-examination; looking into your own personality and actions; reflective

perspec**tive (per- through)** to see through; the way you see something; viewpoint. *a global perspective

speculation – to see ahead; when you guess at how something is going to come out. *She dismissed their ideas as mere speculation.

circumspec**t (circum- around)** watchful and cautious; to look around at all the possibilities.

specter - a visible disembodied ghost; possibly a hallucination?

STUDY CARD 2 — vis, vid - see — LATIN

visible (ible- able) able to be seen.

vista - a pleasing view, especially one seen through a long, narrow opening.

visionary - thinking about (seeing) or planning the future with imagination or wisdom. *a visionary leader.

provid**ent (pro- before)** to see before; to prepare for the future; prudent. *His past money problems made him more careful and provident.

evid**ent (e- out)** plain or obvious; clearly seen or understood.

STUDY CARD 3 — scop, spic – see, view — GREEK

telescop**e (tele- distant)** an optical instrument designed to make distant objects appear nearer,

horoscop**e (horo- hour)** a forecast of a person's future based on the relative positions of the stars and planets at the time of that person's birth.

conspic**uous (con- completely)** standing out; clearly visible.
*He was very thin, with a conspicuous Adam's apple.

auspic**ious** conducive to success; favorable.
*It was not the most auspicious moment to hold an election.

perspic**acious (per- through)** having a ready insight through an understanding of things. intelligent; observant.

Quiz 10 — Latin and Greek Word Roots

Part 1. Write the word for the definition.

| specter | speculation | circumspect | introspection | perspective |

1. _____ to see through; the way you see something; viewpoint.
2. _____ a visible disembodied ghost; possibly a hallucination?
3. _____ watchful and cautious; to look around at all the possibilities.
4. _____ self-examination; looking into your own personality and actions; reflective.
5. _____ to see ahead; when you guess at how something is going to come out.

| vista | visible | evident | provident | visionary |

6. _____ a pleasing view, especially one seen through a long, narrow opening.
7. _____ able to be seen.
8. _____ plain or obvious; clearly seen or understood.
9. _____ to see before; to prepare for the future; prudent.
10. _____ thinking about or planning the future with imagination or wisdom.

| auspicious | perspicacious | conspicuous | telescope | horoscope |

11. _____ an optical instrument designed to make distant objects appear nearer.
12. _____ standing out; clearly visible.
13. _____ conducive to success; favorable.
14. _____ a forecast of a person's future based on the relative positions of the stars and planets at the time of that person's birth.
15. _____ having a ready insight through an understanding of things. intelligent; observant.

Part 2. Write the word root for each word.

| in | per | cir | cum | ible |

1. through _____   2. into _____   3. able _____   4. around _____

| con | e | tele | horo |

5. distant _____   6. hour _____   7. out _____   8. completely _____

WORD CHART LESSON 11

circumference
circumvent
circumspect
circumlocution
circumambulate

peripatetic
peripheral
periscope
perianth
pervade

central
con**centr**ate
con**centr**ic
ec**centr**ic
ego**centr**ic

PART 1 — ***AROUND***

LESSON 11
circum
per/i
AROUND THROUGH
centr
CENTER

- **circum**ference
- **circum**vent — TO GO
- **circum**spect — LOOK
- **circum**locution — TO SPEAK
- **circum**ambulate — WALK

PART 2 — ***AROUND, *THROUGH***

- **peri**patetic
- **peri**pheral
- **peri**scope — TO VIEW
- **peri**anth — FLOWER
- *****per**vade — TO GO

PART 3 — ***CENTER***

- **centr**al
- con**centr**ate
- con**centr**ic
- ec**centr**ic
- ego**centr**ic — SELF

STUDY CARD 1 — circum – around — LATIN

circumference the distance around something, especially a circle.

circumvent (vent- to go) to go around (an obstacle). *I found a way around the obstruction in the road, I circumvented it.

circumspect (spect- look) careful to look at all circumstances and possible consequences; cautious. *They are circumspect in their financial transactions.

circumlocution (locu- to speak) a roundabout or indirect way of speaking; the use of more words than necessary to express an idea.

circumambulate (ambul- to walk) to walk or go around, especially ceremoniously. *They walked slowly and **circumambulated** the outer walls of the temple.

STUDY CARD 2 — per/i – around, through — GREEK

peripatetic - traveling around from place to place; working or based in various places for relatively short periods.

peripheral - around an outer boundary or periphery. *peripheral vision. * A peripheral interest is a secondary or side interest, not your first choice.

periscope (scop- view) used to view around barriers. *typically used in submarines and tanks to see above and around.

perianth (anth- flower) the outer envelope of a flower, including the calyx and corolla.

pervade (vad- to go) to spread or diffuse throughout; permeate; pass through.
*The smell of stale cabbage pervaded the air.

STUDY CARD 3 — centr - center — GREEK

central - located in the center or middle, or the most important part of something. *a central location. *a **central** cause of a problem.

con**centr**ate - focus or center one's attention or mental effort on a particular object or activity. *She tried to concentrate on her homework.

con**centr**ic - having a **common** center; concentric circles or rings. *Which planet has seven colorful concentric rings?

ec**centr**ic - a **person whose behavior or mannerisms are generally regarded as deviating from an accepted norm**; not centered.

ego**centr**ic (ego- self) thinking only of oneself, without regard for the feelings or desires of others; self-centered.

Quiz 11 Latin and Greek Word Roots

Part 1. Write the word for the definition.

| circumlocution | circumference | circumambulate | circumvent | circumspect |

1. _____ to go around (an obstacle).
2. _____ to walk or go around, especially ceremoniously.
3. _____ careful to look at all circumstances and possible consequences.
4. _____ the distance around something, especially a circle.
5. _____ a roundabout or indirect way of speaking; the use of more words than necessary to express an idea.

| perianth | pervade | peripheral | periscope | peripatetic |

6. _____ to spread or diffuse throughout; permeate; pass through.
7. _____ used to view around barriers.
8. _____ around an outer boundary or periphery.
9. _____ the outer envelope of a flower, including the calyx and corolla.
10. _____ traveling around from place to place; working or based in various places for relatively short periods.

| egocentric | eccentric | concentric | concentrate | central |

11. _____ located in the center or middle, or the most important part of something.
12. _____ focus or center one's attention or mental effort on a particular object or activity.
13. _____ having a common center; concentric circles or rings.
14. _____ a person whose behavior or mannerisms are generally regarded as deviating from an accepted norm; not centered.
15. _____ thinking only of oneself, without regard for the feelings or desires of others.

Part 2. Write the word root for each word.

| vad | scop | anth | vent |

1. view _____ 2. to go _____ 3. to go _____ 4. flower _____

| ego | spect | locu | ambul |

5. to walk _____ 6. look _____ 7. to speak _____ 8. self _____

WORD CHART LESSON 12

benevolent
beneficial
beneficiary
benefactor
benefactress

benign
beneficent
benediction
bona fida
bon vivant

eulogy
euphemism
euphoria
euthanasia
eugenics

LESSON 12

ben/e
bon
GOOD, WELL

eu
GOOD, WELL

PART 1 — GOOD

- bene**vol**ent — TO WISH
- bene**fic**ial — TO DO
- bene**fic**iary — TO DO
- bene**fact**or — TO DO
- bene**fact**ress — FEMININE

PART 2 — GOOD, *WELL

- bene**fic**ent — TO DO
- bene**dict**ion — TO SPEAK
- bona**fida** — FAITH
- bon**viv**ant — LIFE
- *benign

PART 3 — GOOD, WELL

- eu**log**y — WORD, DISCOURSE
- eu**phem**ism — SPEECH
- eu**phor**ia — STATE
- eu**thanas**ia — DEATH
- eu**gen**ics — TO PRODUCE

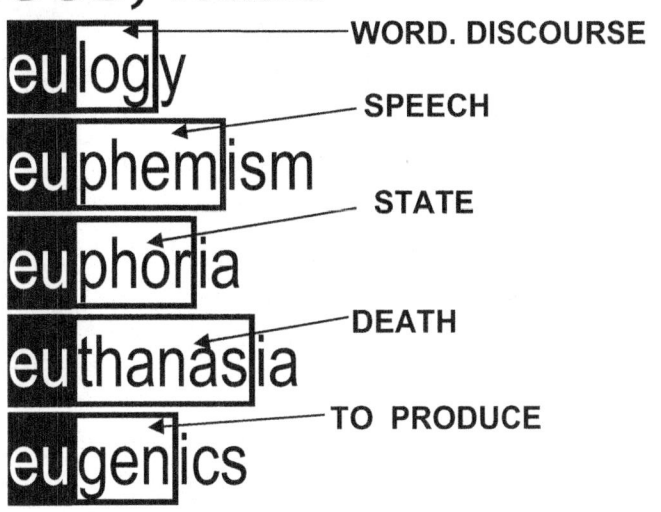

Copyright 2020, Matthew Glavach, Ph.D.

STUDY CARD 1 — **bene – good, well** — LATIN

benevolent **(vol- to wish)** to wish kindness and good will toward others.

beneficial **(fic- to do)** to do something resulting in good. *discoveries beneficial to all. * the beneficial effect of a good economy.

beneficiary **(fic- to do)** a person who gains an advantage (something good) from a trust, will, life insurance policy etc.

benefactor **(or- one who)** one who gives money or other help to a person or good cause; philanthropist. *A donation from a benefactor paid for a new library.

benefactress **(ess- feminine)**; a female benefactor (a somewhat historical term.)

STUDY CARD 2 — **ben/e, bon – good, well** — LATIN

beneficent **(fic- to do)** to do or produce good; especially, performing acts of kindness and charity. *The beneficent couple volunteer at a homeless shelter.

benediction **(dict- speak)** an invocation; to say a blessing, especially, a short blessing. He dismissed the congregation with a BENEDICTION.

bona fida **(fida- faith)** made, done, presented, etc., in good faith; without deception or fraud: authentic.

bon vivant **(viv- life)** someone who enjoys the (good) life; money, dining, traveling, and an active social life.

benign - a term for conditions that present no danger to life or well-being; not harmful. *Benign is the opposite of malignant (bad).

STUDY CARD 3 — **eu – good, well** — GREEK

eulogy **(log- discourse)** a speech or piece of writing that praises someone or something, typically someone who has just died.

euphemism **(phem- speech)** using an agreeable or inoffensive expression for one that may offend. *terms like *passed away* for *dead*; *let go* for *fired*.

euphoria **(phor- state)** a state of well-being and great happiness; elation. *How will you feel when you get your diploma?

euthanasia **(thanas- death)** the practice of intentionally ending a life to relieve pain and suffering.

eugenics **(gen- produce)** the practice of selective breeding of human populations to produce improvement in the population's genetic composition. (No longer practiced.)

Quiz 12   Latin and Greek Word Roots

Part 1. Write the word for the definition.

| benevolent | benefactor | beneficiary | beneficial | benefactress |

1. _____ a female benefactor (a somewhat historical term).
2. _____ to wish kindness and <u>good</u> will toward others.
3. _____ to do something resulting in good.
4. _____ one who gives money or other help to a person or good cause; philanthropist.
5. _____ a person who gains an advantage (something good) from a trust, will, life insurance policy etc.

| bon vivant | benediction | benign | beneficent | bona fida |

6. _____ someone who enjoys the (good) life; money, dining, traveling, and an active social life.
7. _____ a term for conditions that present no danger to life or well-being.
8. _____ made, done, presented, etc., in good faith; without deception or fraud: authentic.
9. _____ an invocation; to say a blessing, especially, a short blessing.
10. _____ to do or produce good; especially, performing acts of kindness and charity.

| euphemism | eulogy | euphoria | eugenics | euthanasia |

11. _____ using an agreeable or inoffensive expression for one that may offend.
12. _____ a state of well-being and great happiness; elation.
13. _____ a speech or piece of writing that praises someone or something, typically someone who has just died.
14. _____ the practice of intentionally ending a life to relieve pain and suffering.
15. _____ the practice or advocacy of selective breeding of human populations to produce improvement in the population's genetic composition.

Part 2. Write the word root for each word.

| fic | dict | fida | ess |

1. **speak** _____   2. **to do** _____   3. **faith** _____   4. **feminine** _____

| viv | phem | phor | thanas |

5. **speech** _____   6. **death** _____   7. **state** _____   8. **life** _____

WORD CHART LESSON 13

malign
malaria
malodorous
malediction
malevolent

misandry
misanthrope
misogynist
misogamist
misology

dystopia
dyspepsia
dystrophy
dyslexia
dysgraphia

LESSON 13

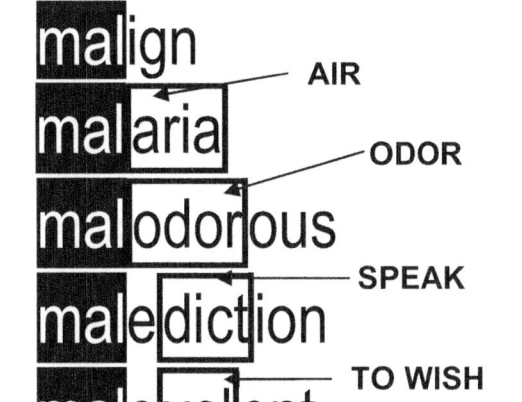

mal — BAD, HATE
mis/o — HATE
dys — BAD, IMPAIRED

PART 1: BAD

- malign
- malaria — AIR
- malodorous — ODOR
- malediction — SPEAK
- malevolent — TO WISH

PART 2: HATE

- misandry — MAN
- misanthrope — MAN
- misogynist — WOMAN
- misogamist — MARRIAGE
- misology — WORD, DISCOURSE

PART 3: BAD, *IMPAIRED

- dystopia — PLACE
- dyspepsia — DIGESTION
- *dystrophy — NOURISHMENT
- *dyslexia — READING
- *dysgraphia — WRITING

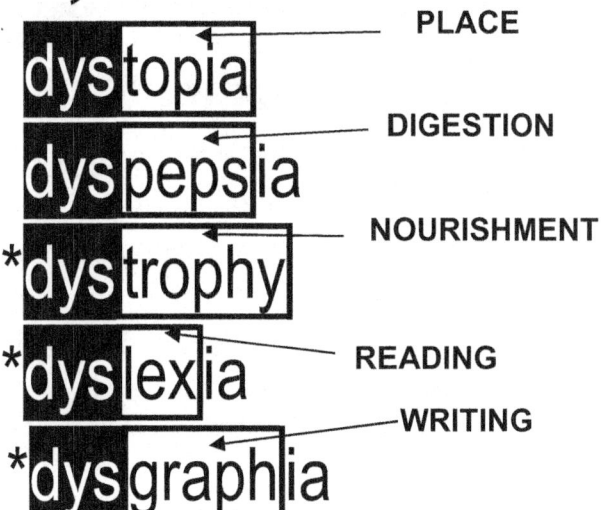

STUDY CARD 1 — **mal – bad, hate** — LATIN

malign to make harmful statements about, especially if untrue.

malaria (aria- bad air) a mosquito-borne infectious disease that affects humans and other animals. *Malaria was once thought to be caused by bad air.

malodorous (odor- odor) bad odor; foul smelling. *Malodorous is a nicer way to say that something stinks.

malediction (dict- to speak) something uttered with the intention of bringing about evil or destruction on someone; a curse.

malevolent (vol- wish) having or showing a wish to do something bad to others; malicious.

STUDY CARD 2 — **mis – hate** — GREEK

misandry (andr- man) dislike of, contempt for, or ingrained prejudice against men.

misanthrope (anthr- mankind) a person who dislikes humankind and avoids human society. *Was *Scrooge* a mean-spirited misanthrope?

misogynist (gyn- women) a person who hates, dislikes, mistrusts, or mistreats women. *When a man hates women, this is an example of **misogyny**.

misogamist (gam-marriage) a person who dislikes marriage; or, **might it be someone** who prefers their independence?

misology (log- discourse) hatred of knowledge, reason, or enlightenment.

STUDY CARD 3 — **dys – mad, impaired** — GREEK

dystopia (topia- place) a community or society that is undesirable or frightening. *It is translated as "not-good place" and is an antonym of utopia,

dyspepsia (peps- digestion) mild indigestion. *Dyspepsia usually resolves itself without any need for medical intervention.

dystrophy (trophy- nourishment) any of various diseases characterized by impaired nutrition, resulting in degeneration of the muscles.

dyslexia (lex- reading) difficulty in learning to read or interpret words, letters, and other symbols. *not affected by general intelligence.

dysgraphia (graph- write) impairment of handwriting characterized chiefly by very poor or often illegible writing or writing that takes great effort.

Quiz 13 — Latin and Greek Roots

Part 1. Write the word for the definition.

| malaria | malodorous | malevolent | malediction | malign |

1. _____ to make harmful statements about, especially if untrue.
2. _____ a mosquito-borne infectious disease that affects humans and other animals.
3. _____ bad odor; foul smelling.
4. _____ having or showing a wish to do something bad to others; malicious.
5. _____ something uttered with the intention of bringing about evil or destruction on someone; a curse.

| misogamist | misology | misogynist | misanthrope | misandry |

6. _____ hatred of knowledge, reason, or enlightenment.
7. _____ a person who dislikes marriage
8. _____ dislike of, contempt for, or ingrained prejudice against men.
9. _____ a person who dislikes humankind and avoids human society.
10. _____ a person who hates, dislikes, mistrusts, or mistreats women.

| dystrophy | dyslexia | dystopia | dyspepsia | dysgraphia |

11. _____ mild indigestion.
12. _____ difficulty in learning to read or interpret words, letters, and other symbols, but not affected by general intelligence.
13. _____ a community or society that is undesirable or frightening.
14. _____ any of various diseases characterized by impaired nutrition, resulting in degeneration of the muscles.
15. _____ impairment of handwriting characterized chiefly by very poor or often illegible writing or writing that takes great effort.

Part 2. Write the word root for each word.

| lex | dict | andr | trophy |

1. reading _____ 2. wish _____ 3. man _____ 4. nourishment _____

| gyn | gam | log | peps |

5. women _____ 6. discourse _____ 7. digestion _____ 8. marriage _____

nomenclature
ig**nom**iny
mo**nom**ial
nominate
mis**nom**er

syn**onym**
ant**onym**
hom**onym**
an**onym**ous
pseud**onym**

neologism
neophyte
neonatal
in**nov**ate
novel

WORD CHART LESSON 14

LESSON 14

nom — NAME, WORD
nym — NAME, WORD
neo — NEW
nov — NEW

PART 1 — NAME

- nomenclature
- WITHOUT — ignominy
- ONE — monomial
- nominate
- WRONG — misnomer

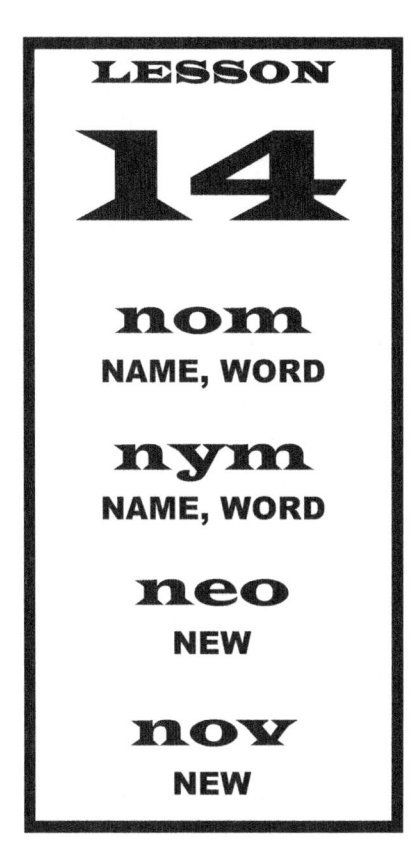

PART 2 — WORD, *NAME

- SAME — synonym
- OPPOSITE — antonym
- SAME — homonym
- WITHOUT — *anonymous
- FALSE — *pseudonym

PART 3 — NEW

- neologism — WORD
- neophyte — TO GROW
- neonatal — BORN
- IN, INTO — innovate
- novel

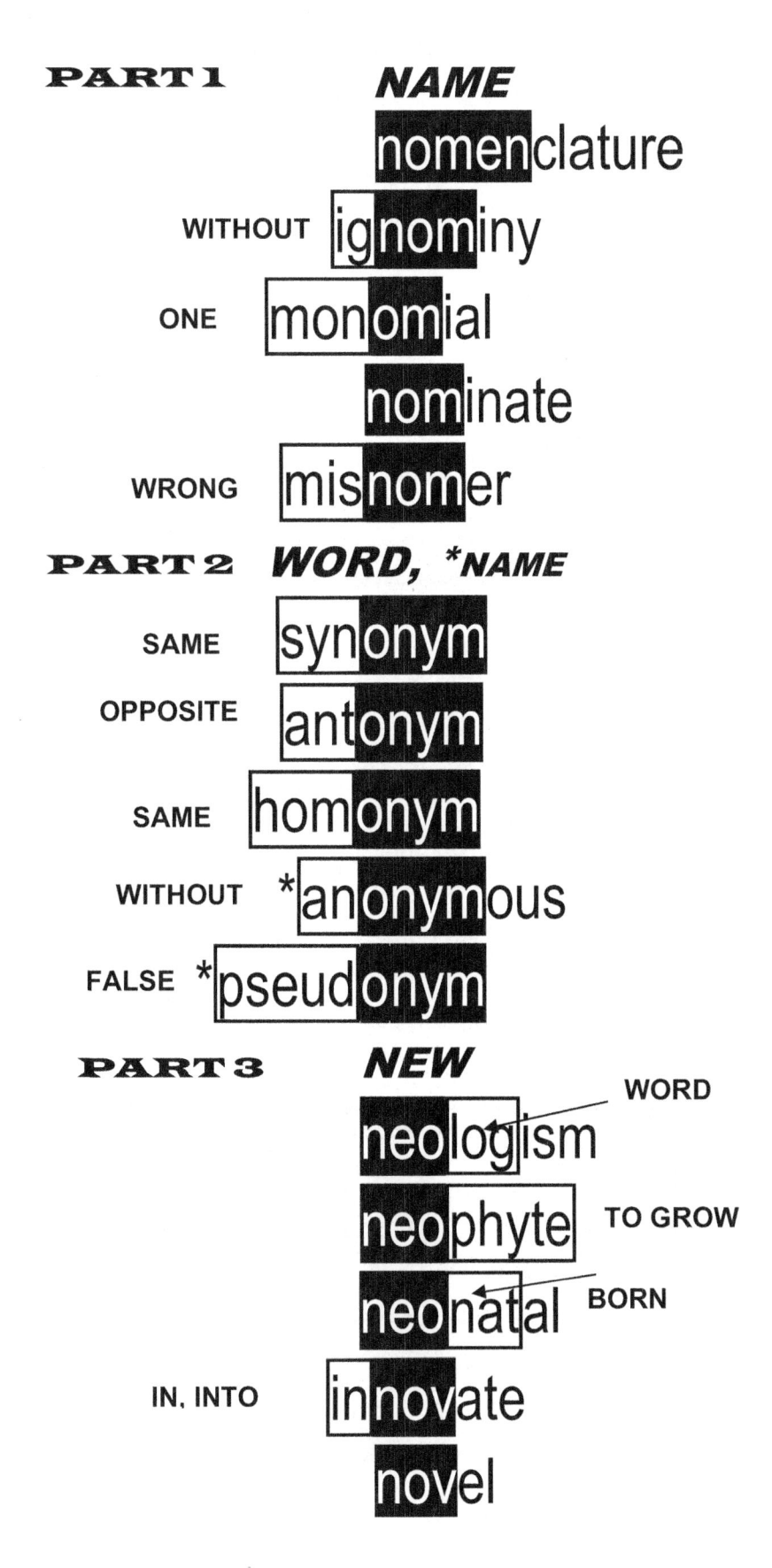

STUDY CARD 1 — **nom – name, word** — GREEK

nomenclature - the body or system of names in a specific field. *the nomenclature of biology.

ignom**iny (ig- without)** the loss of one's good name and reputation; dishonor. *Ignominy is the opposite of esteem.

monom**ial (mon- one)** a mathematical expression consisting of one term or name. *What do *binomial* and *trinomial* mean?

nominate - to officially name someone for an election, job, position, or honor.

misnom**er (mis- bad, wrong)** wrong or unsuitable name; misleading. *Chinese Checkers* is a **misnomer** since the game has nothing to do with China.

STUDY CARD 2 — **o/nym – name, word** — GREEK

synonym **(syn- same)** a word with the same or similar meaning as another word.
* happy, joyful, elated

antonym **(ant- opposite)** a word that has the opposite meaning of another word. *soft - hard; fast - slow

homonym **(homo- same)** a word that sounds the same as another word but has a different spelling and meaning. *feet – feat; fair, fare

anonym**ous (an- without)** without a known or acknowledged name.
*The gift was from an anonymous donor.

pseudonym **(pseudo- false)** a false name; an invented name in place of a real name, especially by a writer. *Samuel Clemens wrote under the pseudonym Mark Twain.

STUDY CARD 3 — **neo, nov – new** — GREEK

neologism **(log- word)** a newly coined word or expression or a new use for an existing word. *Banana Republic. Beatnik. Cyberspace. Nerd.

neophyte **(phyte- to grow)** a beginner; novice a person who is new to a subject, skill, or belief. *The new cooking classes are offered to neophytes only.

neonatal **(nat- born)** a newborn child; especially during the first month after birth. *Neonatal babies are healthier for mothers who did not smoke during pregnancy.

innov**ate (in- into)** to introduce something new; make changes in anything. established. *Why is innovation so important to the automotive industry?

novel - new; fresh; original.

Quiz 14 — Latin and Greek Word Roots

Part 1. Write the word for the definition.

| monomial | nomenclature | nominate | misnomer | ignominy |

1. _____ a **mathematical expression consisting of one term or name.**
2. _____ the loss of one's good name and reputation; dishonor.
3. _____ the body or system of names in a specific field.
4. _____ **to officially name someone for an election, job, position, or honor.**
5. _____ wrong or unsuitable name; misleading.

| antonym | anonymous | homonym | pseudonym | synonym |

6. _____ a word that has the opposite meaning of another word.
7. _____ a false name; an invented name in place of a real name
8. _____ without a known or acknowledged name.
9. _____ a word that sounds the same as another word but has a different spelling and meaning.
10. _____ a word with the same or similar meaning as another word.

| neologism | novel | innovate | neonatal | neophyte |

11. _____ new; fresh; original
12. _____ to introduce something new; make changes in anything established.
13. _____ a newborn child; especially during the first month after birth.
14. _____ a beginner; novice a person who is new to a subject, skill, or belief
15. _____ a newly coined word or expression or a new use for an existing word.

Part 2. Write the word root for each word.

| nov | ig | mis | syn |

1. same _____ 2. wrong _____ 3. new _____ 4. without _____

| anti | same | pseudo | an |

5. false _____ 6. homo _____ 7. without _____ 8. opposite _____

| log | phyte | nat | mon |

9. word _____ 10. grow _____ 11. one _____ 12. born _____

WORD CHART LESSON 15

scribe
de**scribe**
pre**scribe**
in**scribe**
circum**scribe**

script
Scripture
manu**script**
tran**script**
scriptorium

graphology
mono**graph**
lexico**graphy**
graphics
ideo**graphy**

PART 1 — *TO WRITE*

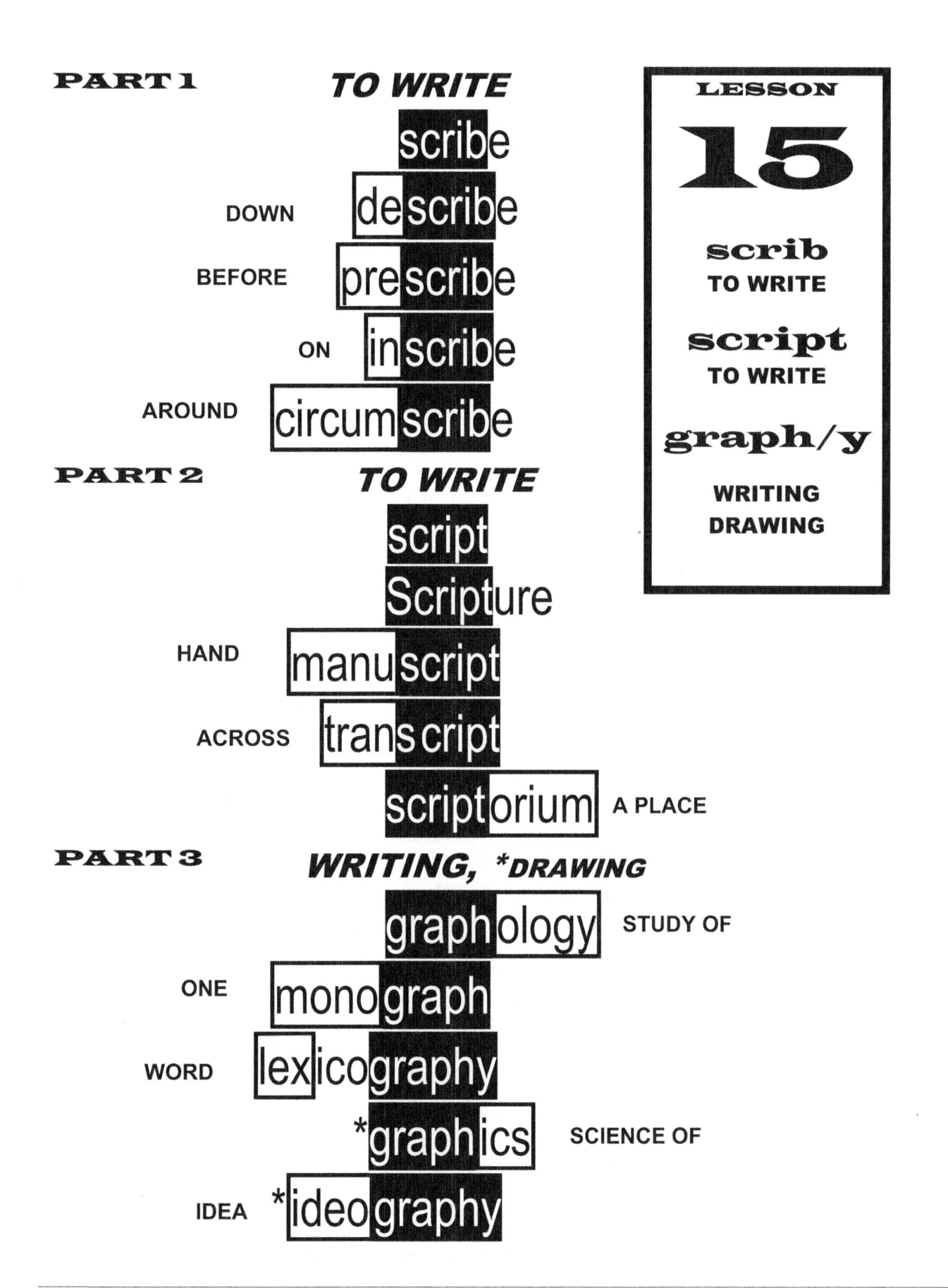

- scribe
- DOWN — describe
- BEFORE — prescribe
- ON — inscribe
- AROUND — circumscribe

LESSON 15

scrib — TO WRITE

script — TO WRITE

graph/y — WRITING DRAWING

PART 2 — *TO WRITE*

- script
- Scripture
- HAND — manuscript
- ACROSS — transcript
- scriptorium — A PLACE

PART 3 — *WRITING, *DRAWING*

- graphology — STUDY OF
- ONE — monograph
- WORD — lexicography
- *graphics — SCIENCE OF
- IDEA — *ideography

STUDY CARD 1 — scrib – to write — LATIN

scribe - a member of a learned class in ancient Israel through New Testament times studying the Scriptures and serving as copyists, editors, etc.

de**scrib**e (de- down) to **say or write down what someone or something is like.** *She described her favorite movie.

pre**scrib**e (pre- before) to write an order for a drug, treatment, or procedure

in**scrib**e (in- on) to **write, engrave, or print as a lasting record.** *She inscribed his name on the gravestone.

circum**scrib**e (circum- around) to draw a line around; encircle. *to **circumscribe** a city on a map.

STUDY CARD 2 — script – to write — LATIN

script - the written text of a play, movie, or broadcast; dialogue. *The play was perfectly scripted.

Scripture - a body of writings considered sacred or authoritative. *the books of the Bible; a passage from the Bible.

manu**script** (manu- hand) 1.a book, document, or music written by hand rather than typed or printed. 2.an author's text that has not yet been published.

tran**script** (trans- change) 1.a written copy of spoken material. 2.an official record of a student's work, showing courses taken and grades achieved.

scriptorium (orium- a place for) a place set apart for writing, especially one in a monastery where manuscripts were copied.

STUDY CARD 3 — graph/y – writing, drawing — GREEK

graphology (ology- study of) the study of handwriting, especially for determining a person's character.

mono**graph** (mono- single) a detailed written study of a single specialized subject. *a series of monographs on the role of phonics in learning to read.

lexico**graphy** (lex- word) the writing or compiling of dictionaries. *Merriam-Webster was a famous lexicographer and he was also famous for?

graphics (ics- skill) the products of drawing (graphic arts), especially commercial design or illustration.

ideo**graphy** (ideo- idea) the representation of ideas using graphic symbols.

Quiz 15 — Latin and Greek Word Roots

Part 1. Write the word for the definition.

| scribe | prescribe | circumscribe | inscribe | describe |

1. _____ to draw a line around; encircle
2. _____ to write an order for a drug, treatment, or procedure.
3. _____ to **write, engrave, or print as a lasting record.**
4. _____ to **say or write down what someone or something is like.**
5. _____ a member of a learned class in ancient Israel through New Testament times studying the Scriptures and serving as copyists, editors, etc.

| manuscript | script | scriptorium | transcript | Scripture |

6. _____ a book, document, or music written by hand rather than typed or printed.
7. _____ the written text of a play, movie, or broadcast; dialogue.
8. _____ a written copy of spoken material.
9. _____ a place set apart for writing
10. _____ a body of writings considered sacred or authoritative.

| graphics | graphology | monograph | lexicography | ideography |

11. _____ the writing or compiling of dictionaries.
12. _____ The representation of ideas using graphic symbols.
13. _____ the study of handwriting, especially for determining a person's character.
14. _____ the products of drawing.
15. _____ a detailed written study of a single specialized subject.

Part 2. Write the word root for each word.

| scrib | de | pre | in |

1. on _____   2. to write _____   3. before _____   4. down _____

| circum | manu | trans | orium |

5. hand _____   6. change _____   7. a place for _____   8. around _____

| ology | mono | lex | ideo |

9. idea _____   10. study of _____   11. single _____   12. word _____

65

Copyright 2020, Matthew Glavach, Ph.D.

WORD CHART LESSON 16

lingual
uni**lingu**al
bi**lingu**al
linguist
linguistics

dia**log**ue
pro**log**ue
epi**log**ue
mono**log**ue
tri**log**y

literary
literature
literate
il**liter**ate
al**liter**ation

LESSON 16

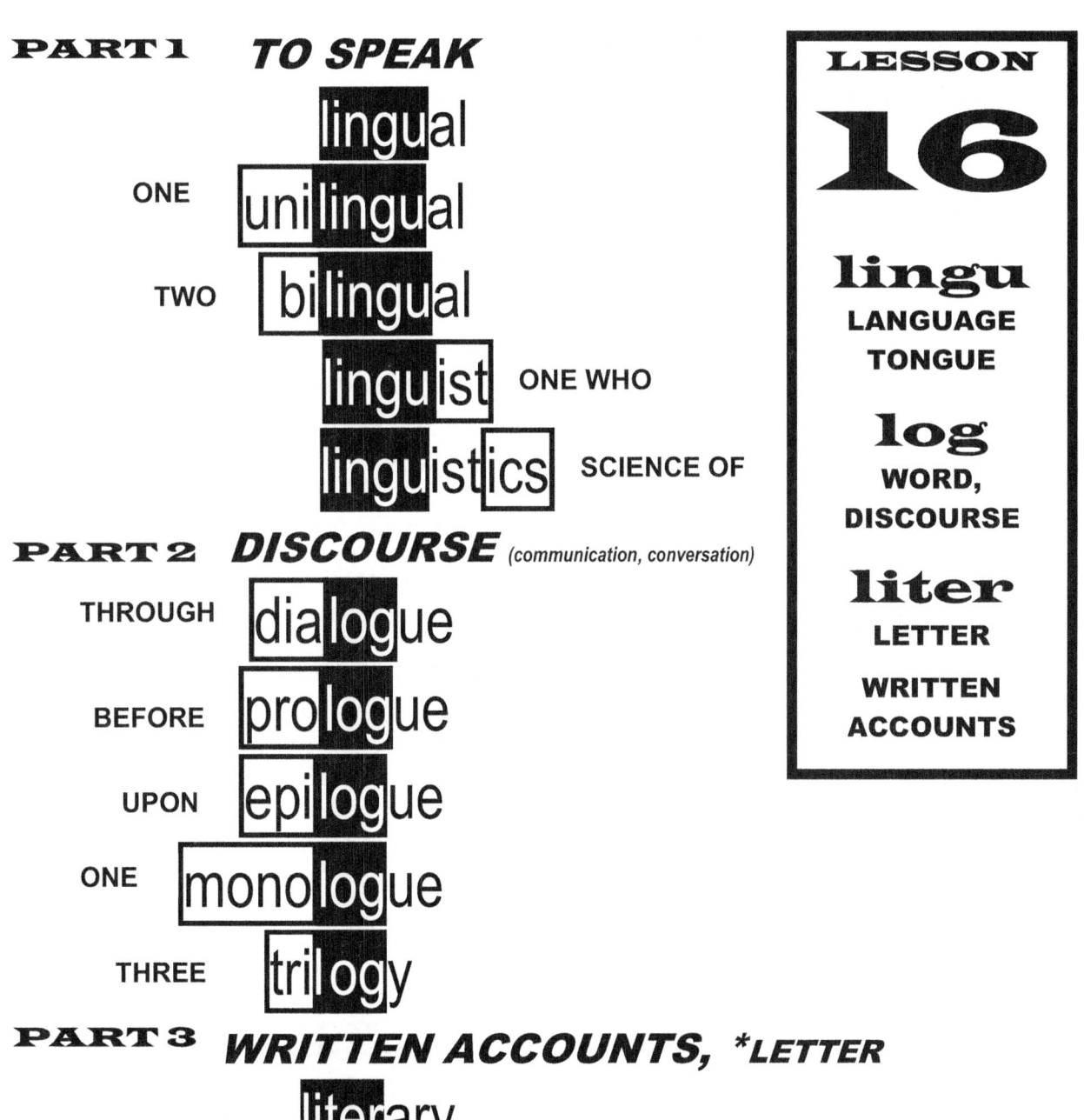

lingu — LANGUAGE, TONGUE
log — WORD, DISCOURSE
liter — LETTER, WRITTEN ACCOUNTS

PART 1 — TO SPEAK

- lingual
- unilingual — ONE
- bilingual — TWO
- linguist — ONE WHO
- linguistics — SCIENCE OF

PART 2 — DISCOURSE (communication, conversation)

- dialogue — THROUGH
- prologue — BEFORE
- epilogue — UPON
- monologue — ONE
- trilogy — THREE

PART 3 — WRITTEN ACCOUNTS, *LETTER

- literary
- literature
- literate
- illiterate — NO
- *alliteration — TOWARD

STUDY CARD 1 — **lingu – to speak** — LATIN

lingual - 1.relating to the tongue. 2.relating to speech or language.

uni**lingu**al (uni- one) speaking just one language. *If you only speak English and no other language, you are unilingual.

bi**lingu**al (bi- two) able to speak two languages with the facility of a native speaker.

linguist (ist- one who) a person accomplished in languages; especially one who speaks several languages.

linguistics (ics- science of) the science of language. *includess phonetics, phonology, morphology, syntax, semantics, pragmatics, and historical linguistics.

STUDY CARD 2 — **log – word, discourse** — GREEK

dia**log**ue (dia- through) through discourse; a conversation between two or more people as a feature of a book, play, or movie. *The book had a series of dialogues.

pro**log**ue (pro- before) a part that comes before (introduction) a play, story, or long **poem.**

epi**log**ue (epi- upon) a section or speech at the end of a book or play that comments upon what has happened. *The book's title is revealed in the epilogue.

mono**log**ue (mono- one) a speech presented by one person. *The opening discourse by the late-night talk show host was a monologue.

tri**log**y (tri- three) a series or group of three plays, novels, operas, etc., that, although individually complete, are closely related.

STUDY CARD 3 — **liter – letter, written accounts** — LATIN

literary - the writing, study, or content of literature, especially of the kind valued for quality of form. *the great literary works of the nineteenth century.

literature - written works, especially those considered of superior or lasting artistic merit.

literate - able to read and write.

il**liter**ate (il- not) not able to read or write.

al**liter**ation (al- toward) when words have the same first consonant letter/sound close together. *a better batter makes baseball better. "Make an alliteration of your own."

Quiz 16 Latin and Greek Word Roots

Part 1. Write the word for the definition.

| bilingual | linguist | lingual | linguistics | unilingual |

1. _____ speaking just one language.
2. _____ a person accomplished in languages
3. _____ able to speak two languages with the facility of a native speaker.
4. _____ 1.relating to the tongue. 2.relating to speech or language.
5. _____ the science of language.

| monologue | trilogy | epilogue | prologue | dialogue |

6. _____ a series or group of three plays, novels, operas, etc.
7. _____ a speech
8. _____ a speech presented by one person.
9. _____ a part that comes before (introduction) a play, story, or long **poem.**
10. _____ through discourse; a conversation between two or more people as a feature of a book, play, or movie.

| literary | illiterate | alliteration | literate | literature |

11. _____ able to read and write.
12. _____ the writing, study, or content of literature, especially of the kind valued for quality of form.
13. _____ not able to read or write.
14. _____ when a number of words having the same first consonant letter/sound occur close together
15. _____ written works, especially those considered of superior or lasting artistic merit.

Part 2. Write the word root for each word.

| uni | bi | ist | ics |

1. one who _____   2. one _____   3. science of _____   4. two _____

| dia | pro | epi | mono |

5. upon _____   6. one _____   7. before _____   8. through _____

Copyright 2020, Matthew Glavach, Ph.D.

WORD CHART LESSON 17

dictate
dictator
ab**dic**ate
in**dict**
juris**dict**ion

dictum
ver**dict**
contra**dict**
e**dict**
vale**dict**orian

e**locu**tion
circum**locu**tion
col**loqu**ial
loquacious
soli**loqu**y

LESSON 17

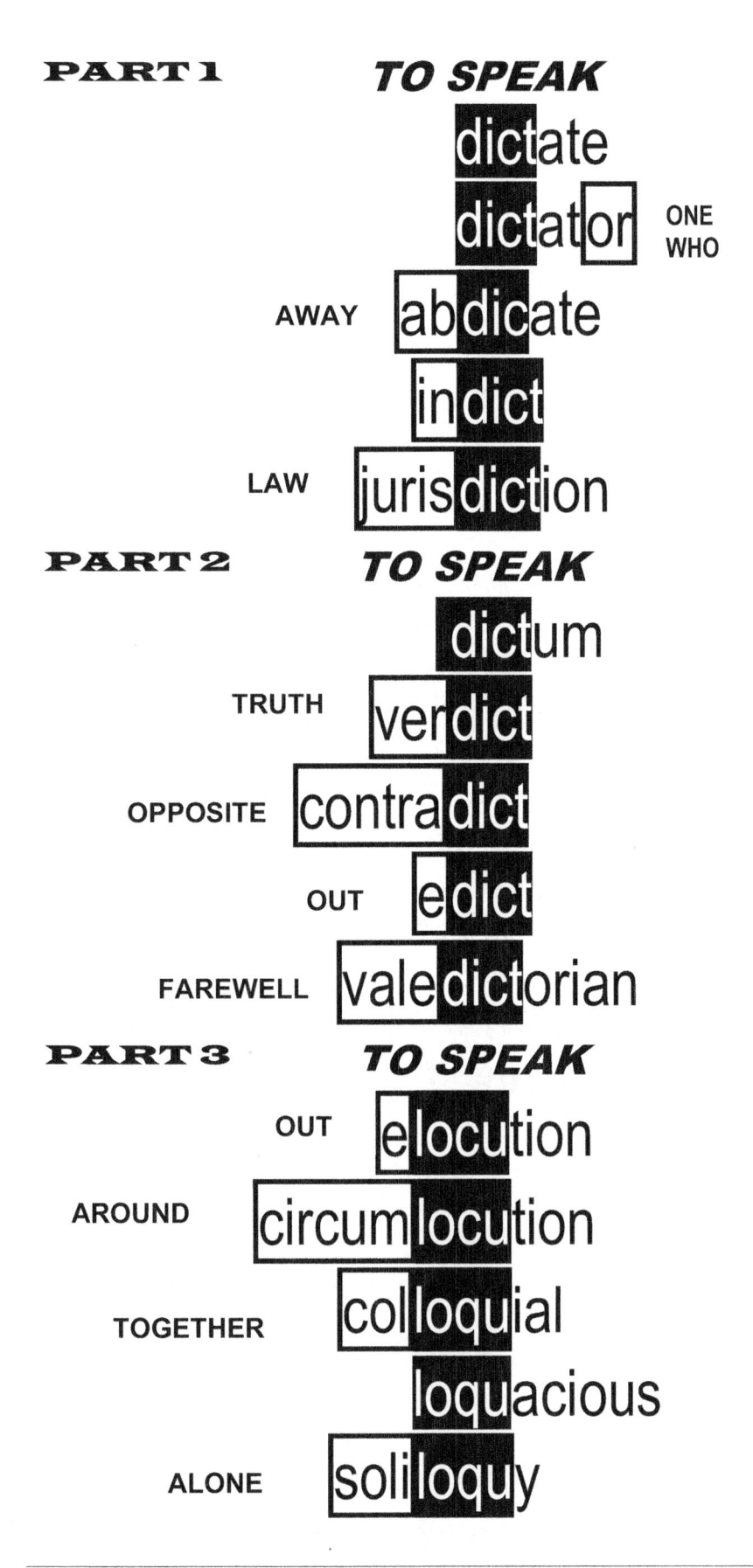

dict — TO SPEAK

locu / loqu — TO SPEAK

PART 1 — TO SPEAK

- dictate
- dictator — ONE WHO
- AWAY — abdicate
- indict
- LAW — jurisdiction

PART 2 — TO SPEAK

- dictum
- TRUTH — verdict
- OPPOSITE — contradict
- OUT — edict
- FAREWELL — valedictorian

PART 3 — TO SPEAK

- OUT — elocution
- AROUND — circumlocution
- TOGETHER — colloquial
- loquacious
- ALONE — soliloquy

STUDY CARD 1 — dict – to speak — LATIN

dictate - to speak authoritatively; prescribe. *the council's attempts to dictate policy. *the dictates of fashion.

dictator (or- one who) one who rules (speaks) with total power over a country, typically one who has obtained control by force.

abdicate (ab- away) 1. (of a monarch) renounce one's throne. 2. fail to fulfill or undertake a responsibility or duty. *to abdicate one's duties.

indict (in- into) formally accuse (speak) of or charge with a serious crime. *His former manager was indicted for fraud.

jurisdiction (juris- law) the extent of the power to make legal decisions and judgments. *Jurisdiction over a vessel on the high seas resides with the State to which the vessel belongs.

STUDY CARD 2 — dict – to speak — LATIN

dictum - a formal pronouncement from an authoritative source; a mandate.

verdict (ver- truth) an opinion or decision made after judging the truthfulness of the facts given. *The foreman of the jury passed the verdict to the judge.

contradict (contra- opposite) statements, ideas, or features of a situation that are opposed (opposite) to one another. *The witness contradicted the driver's testimony.

edict (e- out) an official order or proclamation spoken by a person in authority. *The king issued an edict that all of his subjects pay a fair tax.

valedictorian (vale- farewell) a student, typically having the highest academic achievements of the class, who delivers the farewell valedictory speech at graduation.

STUDY CARD 3 — loqu, locu – to speak — LATIN

elocution (e- out) speaking out; the art of public speaking or reading; well spoken; eloquent.

circumlocution (circum- around) a roundabout, longwinded or evasive way of speaking. *Politicians are experts in circumlocution.

colloquial (col- together) speaking together informally; ordinary or familiar conversation; everyday language.

loquacious - tending to be very talkative; wordy. *Sarah was loquacious, never lost for words.

soliloquy (soli- alone) 1. talking to oneself. 2. The part of the drama where the character talks to herself. *She ends the scene with a soliloquy.

Quiz 17 — Latin and Greek Word Roots

Part 1. Write the word for the definition.

| dictator | indict | jurisdiction | abdicate | dictate |

1. _____ to speak authoritatively; prescribe.
2. _____ one who rules (speaks) with total power over a country.
3. _____ formally accuse (speak) of or charge with a serious crime.
4. _____ the extent of the power to make legal decisions and judgments.
5. _____ 1. (of a monarch) renounce one's throne. 2. fail to fulfill or undertake a responsibility or duty.

| verdict | edict | dictum | valedictorian | contradict |

6. _____ a student, typically having the highest academic achievements of the class, who delivers the farewell speech at graduation.
7. _____ an official order or proclamation spoken by a person in authority.
8. _____ an opinion or decision made after judging the truthfulness of the facts given.
9. _____ a formal pronouncement from an authoritative source; a mandate.
10. _____ statements, ideas, or features of a situation that are opposed (opposite) to one another.

| elocution | colloquial | loquacious | soliloquy | circumlocution |

11. _____ speaking out; the art of public speaking or reading.
12. _____ a roundabout, longwinded or evasive way of speaking.
13. _____ speaking together informally; ordinary or familiar conversation
14. _____ tending to be very talkative; wordy.
15. _____ talking to oneself.

Part 2. Write the word root for each word.

| or | ab | juris | ver |

1. away _____   2. truth _____   3. law _____   4. one who _____

| contra | vale | circum | soli- |

5. around _____   6. alone _____   7. farewell _____   8. opposite _____

WORD CHART LESSON 18

tele**phon**e
mega**phon**e
sym**phon**y
eu**phon**y
caco**phon**y

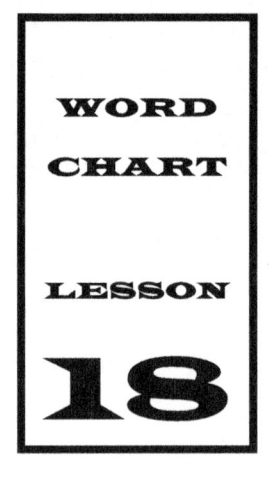

irre**voc**able
vocation
con**voc**ation
ad**voc**ate
equi**voc**al

pro**voc**ative
in**vok**e
re**vok**e
con**vok**e
e**vok**e

LESSON 18

phon — SOUND
voc — TO CALL, VOICE

PART 1 — *SOUND*

- DISTANT — **tele**phone
- LARGE — **mega**phone
- TOGETHER — **sym**phony
- GOOD — **eu**phony
- HARSH — **caco**phony

PART 2 — *TO CALL, *VOICE*

- NOT / BACK — **ir**re**vocable**
- — vocation
- TOGETHER — **con**vocation
- TO — ***ad**vocate
- EQUAL — ***equi**vocal

PART 3 — *TO CALL*

- FORTH — **pro**vocative
- — **in**voke
- BACK — **re**voke
- TOGETHER — **con**voke
- OUT — **e**voke

STUDY CARD 1 — phon – sound — GREEK

telephone (tele- distant) a device for transmitting speech sounds or other data from distant locations. *a telephone call; a cellphone

megaphone (mega- large) a large, cone-shaped device designed to amplify and direct sound.

symphony (sym- together) 1. a harmony of sounds or colors. 2. a concert by a symphony orchestra.

euphony (eu- good) having a good or agreeable sound especially through a harmonious combination of words. *The singer put euphony before lyrics.

cacophony (caco- harsh) harsh or disagreeable sounds; discord; dissonance. *a cacophony of deafening car alarms.

STUDY CARD 2 — voc – to call, voice — LATIN

irrevocable (ir- not; re- back) not able to be called back; changed; or recovered; final; irreversible. *an irrevocable trust.

vocation - a calling or strong interest to enter a certain profession, trade, etc.

convocation (con- together) 1. a calling together of a large group of people. *a formal ceremony at a college or university, as for the conferring of awards.

advocate (ad- to) to speak or write in favor of something. *He was an untiring advocate of academic reform.

equivocal (equi- equal) having more than one meaning and often intended to deceive or mislead. *The defendant's alibi is equivocal; the jury will disregard it almost instantly.

STUDY CARD 3 — voc, vok – to call — LATIN

provocative (pro- forth) to call forth; to provoke, excite, or stimulate. *a stimulating discussion or a provocative remark.

invoke - 1. to call on or appeal to for support or assistance. 2. to initiate or put into use.

revoke (re- back) to call back or cancel as in a license, permit, etc.

convoke (con- together) to call together for a meeting or assembly.

evoke (e- out) bring out or recall to the conscious mind. *The sight of their old house evoked pleasant memories of childhood.

Quiz 18 — Latin and Greek Word Roots

Part 1. Write the word for the definition.

telephone	megaphone	euphony	cacophony	symphony

1. _____ a harmony of sounds or colors; a concert by an orchestra.
2. _____ harsh or disagreeable sounds; discord; dissonance.
3. _____ a device for transmitting speech sounds or other data from distant locations.
4. _____ a large, cone-shaped device designed to amplify and direct sounds.
5. _____ having a good or agreeable sound especially through a harmonious combination of words.

advocate	equivocal	convocation	vocation	irrevocable

6. _____ not able to be called back; changed; or recovered; final; irreversible.
7. _____ to speak or write in favor of something.
8. _____ having more than one meaning and often intended to deceive or mislead.
9. _____ a calling together of a large group of people.
10. _____ a calling or strong interest to enter a certain profession, trade, etc.

provocative	evoke	invoke	convoke	revoke

11. _____ bring out or recall to the conscious mind.
12. _____ to call forth; to provoke, excite, or stimulate.
13. _____ to call back or cancel
14. _____ to call together for a meeting or assembly.
15. _____ 1. to call on or appeal to for support or assistance. 2. to initiate or put into.

Part 2. Write the word root for each word.

tele	mega	sym	eu

1. good _____   2. distant _____   3. together _____   4. large _____

caco	ir	con	equi

5. not _____   6. harsh _____   7. equal _____   8. together _____

pro	re	voc	phon

9. back _____   10. sound _____   11. forth _____   12. to call _____

WORD CHART LESSON 19

biblio**phil**e
philosopher
philanthropist
philology
philatelist

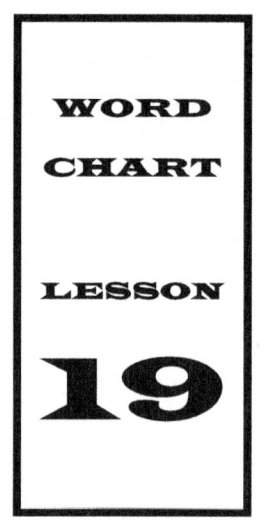

acro**phobia**
agora**phobia**
hydro**phobia**
arachno**phobia**
xeno**phobia**

fable
af**fab**le
inef**fab**le
fame
in**fam**ous

LESSON 19

phil — LOVE
phobia — FEAR
fab
fam — SPEAK

PART 1 — *LOVE*

- BOOK — **biblio**phile
- **philo**sopher — WISDOM (soph), MAN (anthrop)
- **phil**anthropist
- **phil**ology — STUDY
- **phil**atelist

PART 2 — *FEAR*

- HIGH — acro**phobia**
- MARKETPLACE — agora**phobia**
- WATER — hydro**phobia**
- SPIDER — arachno**phobia**
- FOREIGN — xeno**phobia**

PART 3 — *SPEAK*

- fable
- affable
- NOT — ineffable
- fame
- NOT — infamous

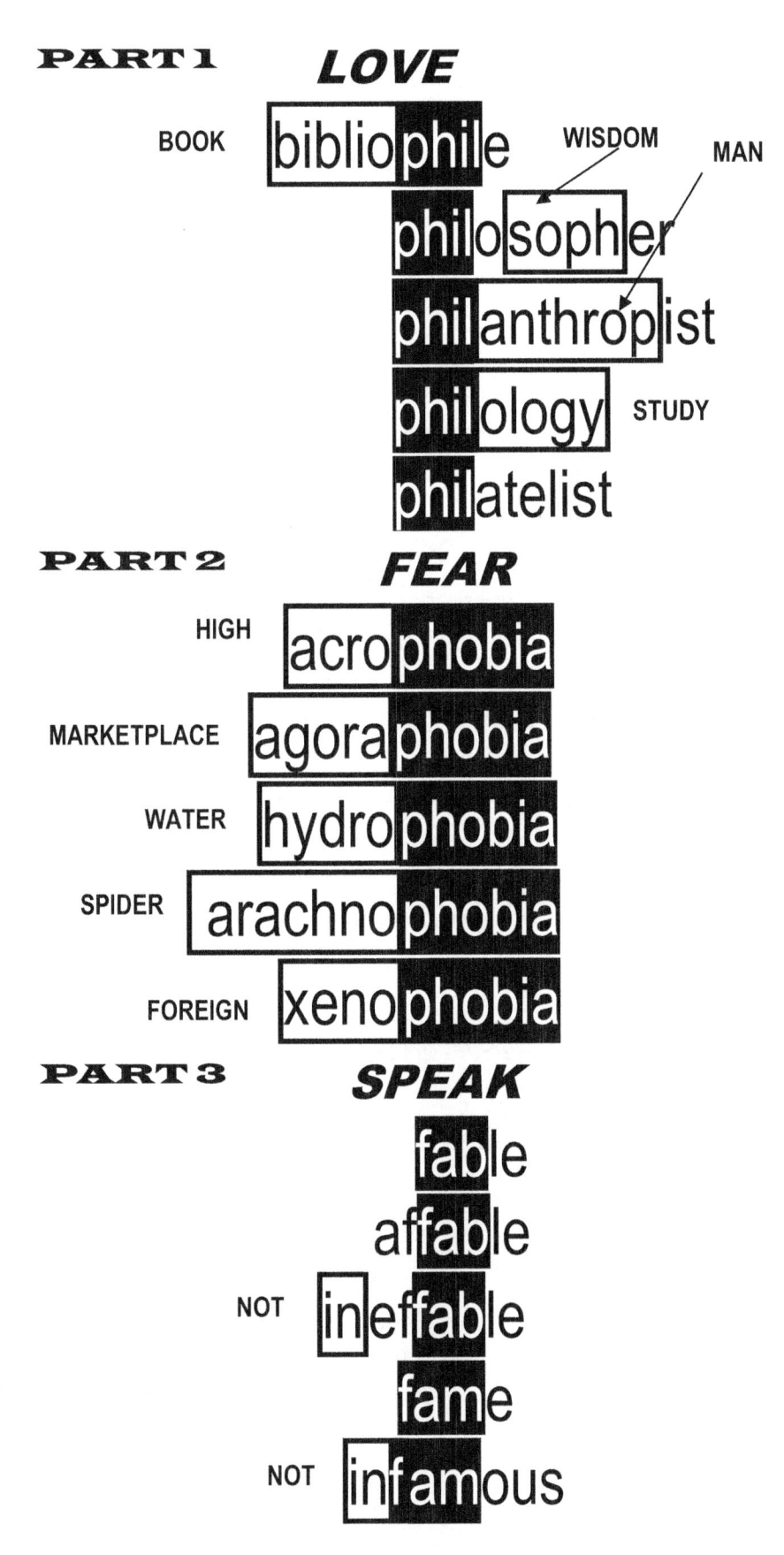

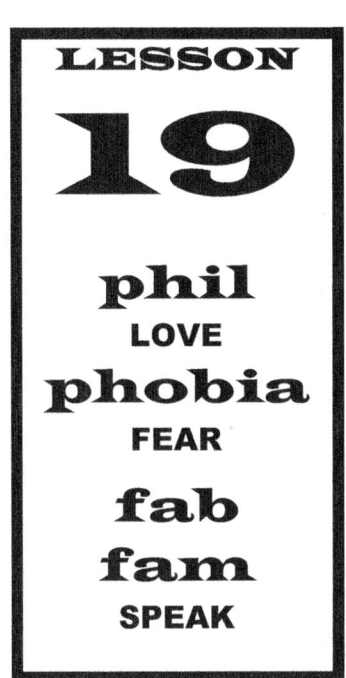

STUDY CARD 1 — phil – love *(GREEK)*

bibliophil**e (biblio- book)** a person who collects or has a great love of books.

philosopher **(soph- wisdom)** a person who loves learning and offers views or theories on profound questions; has great wisdom.

philanthropist **(anthrop- mankind)** 1. a lover of mankind. 2. a person who promotes the welfare of others, especially by the generous donation of money.

philology **(ology- study)** 1. a love of literature and learning. 2. the study of the structure, historical development, and relationships of a language.

philatelist - one who loves or enjoys collecting or studying stamps.

STUDY CARD 2 — phobia – fear *(GREEK)*

acrophobia **(acro- high)** extreme or irrational fear of heights.

agoraphobia **(agora- marketplace)** extreme fear entering open or crowded places, of leaving one's own home, or of being in places from which escape is difficult.

hydrophobia **(hydro- water)** an irrational fear of water, to drink or to swim in.

arachnophobia **(arachno- spiders)** extreme or irrational fear of spiders.

xenophobia **(xeno- foreign)** a fear of or prejudice against people from other countries. *the resurgence of racism and xenophobia.

STUDY CARD 3 — fab, fam – speak *(GREEK)*

fable - a short story, typically with animals speaking as characters, conveying a moral. *the fable of the sick lion and the wary fox.

af**fab**le - friendly, good-natured, or easy to talk to. *an affable and agreeable companion

inef**fab**le **(in- not)** not capable of being expressed or described in words. * the natural beauty of Lake Tahoe.

fame **(fam- speak)** being known or talked about by many people, especially because of notable achievements. *He was inducted into the baseball Hall of Fame.

in**fam**ous **(in- not)** not known for some good quality or deeds.

*an infamous war criminal

Quiz 19   Latin and Greek Word Roots

Part 1. Write the word for the definition.

| philosopher | philanthropist | philology | philatelist | bibliophile |

1. _____ a person who collects or has a great love of books.
2. _____ ¹·a love of literature and learning. ²·the study of the structure, historical development, and relationships of a language.
3. _____ a lover of mankind; a person who promotes the welfare of others, especially by the generous donation of money.
4. _____ one who loves or enjoys collecting or studying stamps.
5. _____ a person who loves learning and offers views or theories on profound questions; has great wisdom.

| acrophobia | agoraphobia | hydrophobia | arachnophobia | xenophobia |

6. _____ **an irrational fear of water, to drink or to swim** in.
7. _____ extreme or irrational fear of spiders.
8. _____ extreme or irrational fear of heights.
9. _____ a fear of or prejudice against people from other countries.
10. _____ extreme fear entering open or crowded places, of leaving one's own home, or of being in places from which escape is difficult.

| ineffable | fame | infamous | fable | affable |

11. _____ friendly, good-natured, or easy to talk to.
12. _____ a short story, typically with animals speaking as characters, conveying a moral.
13. _____ not capable of being expressed or described in words.
14. _____ not known for some good quality or deeds.
15. _____ being known or talked about by many people, especially because of notable achievements.

Part 2. Write the word root for each word.

| biblio | soph | anthrop | acro |

1. high _____ 2. book _____ 3. mankind _____ 4. wisdom _____

| agora | hydro | arachno | xeno |

5. water _____ 6. spiders _____ 7. foreign _____ 8. marketplace _____

biology
biotic
a**bio**tic
biome
amphi**bi**an

WORD CHART LESSON 20

sym**bio**sis
bioluminescence
biodegradable
biography
auto**bio**graphy

sur**viv**e
re**viv**e
viviparous
ovo**viv**iparous
vivacious

LESSON 20

bi/o — LIFE
viv/i — LIFE

PART 1 — *LIFE*

- **biology** — STUDY OF
- **biotic** — RELATING TO
- **abiotic** — WITHOUT / RELATING TO
- **biome** — MASS
- **amphibian** — BOTH

PART 2 — *LIFE*

- **symbiosis** — TOGETHER
- **bioluminescence** — LIGHT
- **biodegradable** — DOWN / STEP
- **biography** — WRITTEN
- **autobiography** — SELF / WRITTEN

PART 3 — *LIFE*

- **survive** — BEYOND
- **revive** — BACK
- **viviparous** — TO PRODUCE
- **ovoviviparous** — EGG / TO PRODUCE
- **vivacious**

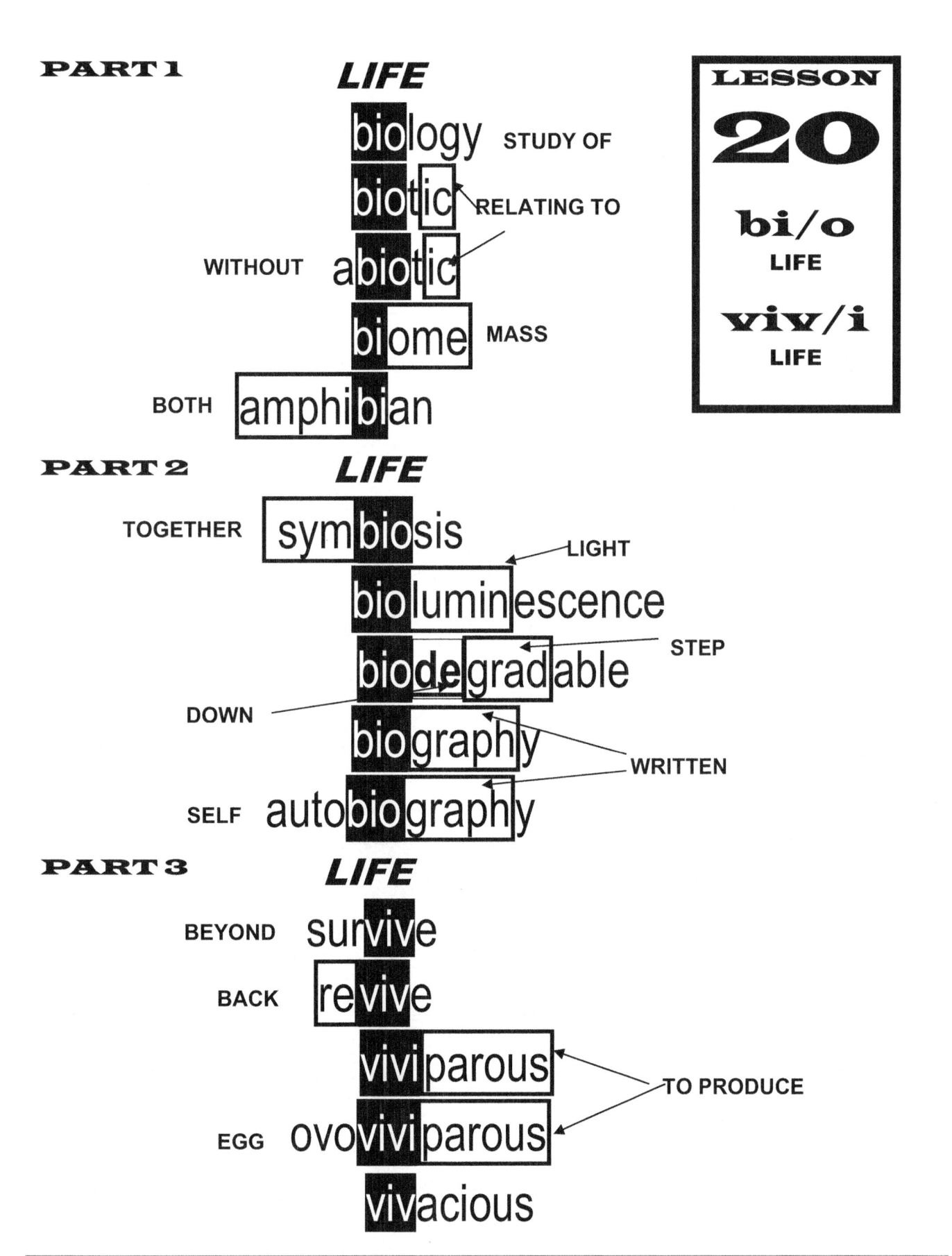

STUDY CARD 1 — **bio - life** — GREEK

biology **(logy- study of)** the scientific study of life.

*If students in biology class are studying amphibians; what are they studying about?

biotic **(ic– relating to)** relating to life.

a**bio**tic **(a- without)** without life; absence of life.

biome **(ome- mass)** the mass or community of plants and animals living in a given region, grassland, desert, etc.

amphi**bi**an **(amphi- both)**- an animal, such as a frog, that can live both on land and in water; also, vehicles. *An amphibious vehicle can travel on land and in water.

STUDY CARD 2 — **bio - life** — GREEK

sym**bio**sis **(sym- together)** two unlike species living together for mutual benefit.

bioluminescence **(lumin- light)** living organisms that produce light.

biodegradable **(de- down; grad- step)** able to break down or decay naturally, by living organisms. Plastics are not biodegradable.

biography **(graph- written)** the story of one's life written by another; a book about a person's life. *He enjoys reading biographies of famous people.

auto**bio**graphy **(auto- self)** the story of one's life written by oneself.

STUDY CARD 3 — **vi, viv - life** — LATIN

sur**viv**e **(sur- beyond)** to live beyond. to continue to live or exist, especially in spite of danger or hardship. Did he survive the accident?

re**viv**e **(re- back)** to bring back to life. The lifeguard revived the drowning victim.

viviparous **(parous- to produce)** producing live young rather than eggs; most mammals

ovo**viv**iparous **(ovo- egg)** producing eggs that hatch internally, fishes, reptiles, etc.

vivacious - lively and spirited; animated. Are cheerleaders vivacious?

Quiz 20 — Latin and Greek Word Roots

Part 1. Write the word for the definition.

| biotic | abiotic | biology | amphibian | biome |

1. _____ relating to life.
2. _____ the scientific study of life.
3. _____ without life; absence of life.
4. _____ the mass or community of plants and animals living in a given region.
5. _____ an animal, such as a frog, that can live both on land and in water; also, vehicles.

| biodegradable | bioluminescence | biography | symbiosis | autobiography |

6. _____ two unlike species living together for mutual benefit.
7. _____ the story of one's life written by oneself.
8. _____ the story of one's life written by another; a book about a person's life.
9. _____ living organisms that produce light.
10. _____ able to break down or decay naturally, by living organisms.

| survive | revive | viviparous | ovoviviparous | vivacious |

11. _____ to live beyond; to continue to live or exist.
12. _____ to bring back to life.
13. _____ producing live young rather than eggs; most mammals
14. _____ producing eggs that hatch internally, fishes, reptiles, etc.
15. _____ lively and spirited; animated.

Part 2. Write the word root for each word.

| logy | ome | amphi | sym |

1. mass _____ 2. study of _____ 3. together _____ 4. both _____

| de | grad | graph | sur |

5. written _____ 6. step _____ 7. down _____ 8. beyond _____

| re | parous | egg | viv, bio |

9. ovo _____ 10. back _____ 11. life _____ 12. produce _____

WORD CHART LESSON 21

genetics
gender
pro**gen**y
con**gen**ital
genocide

genesis
generate
endo**gen**ous
exo**gen**ous
neuro**gen**esis

genre
generic
carcino**gen**ic
hetero**gen**eous
homo**gen**ous

LESSON 21

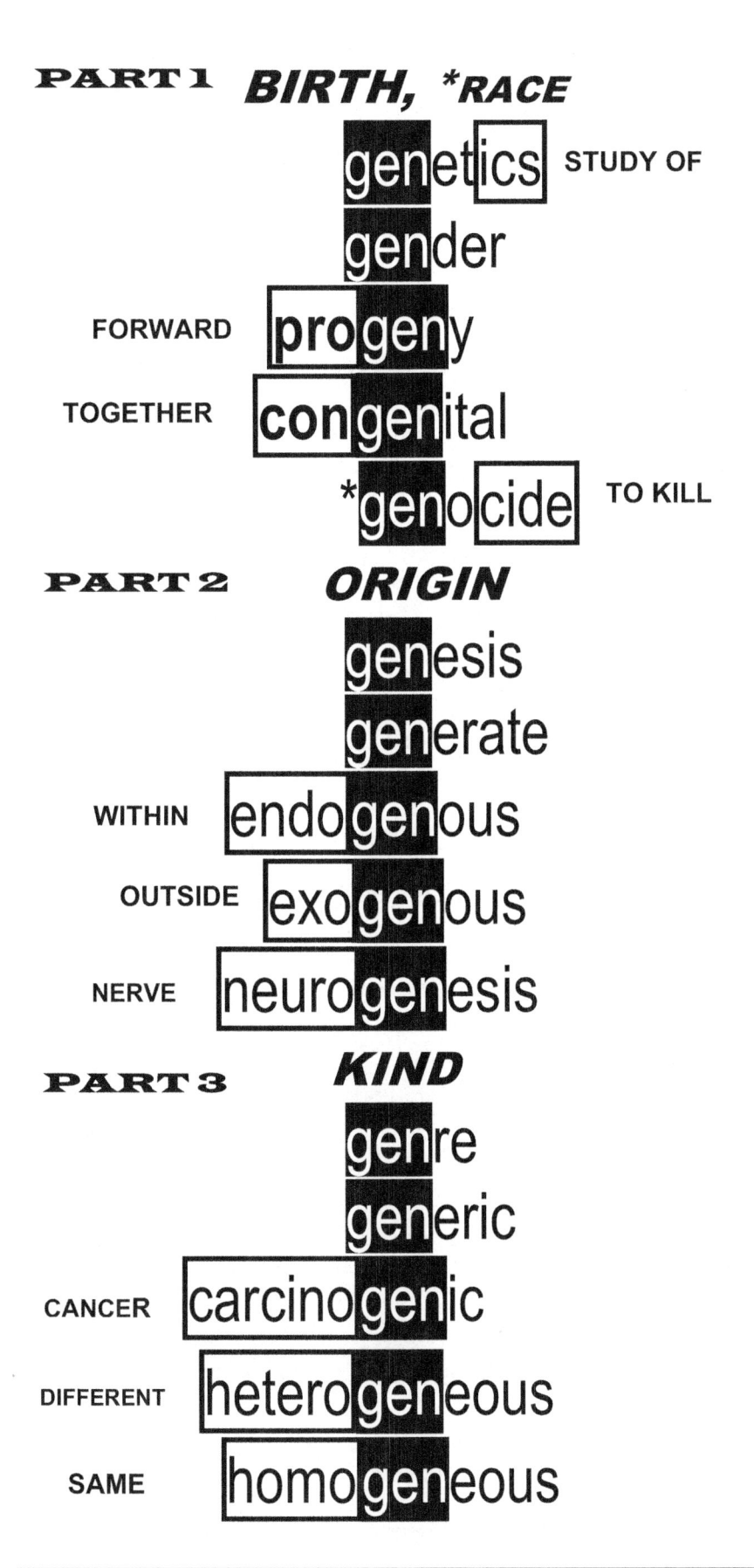

gen

BIRTH, RACE

ORIGIN

KIND

PART 1 — *BIRTH, *RACE*

- gene**t**ics — STUDY OF
- gender
- **pro**geny — FORWARD
- **con**genital — TOGETHER
- *geno**cide** — TO KILL

PART 2 — *ORIGIN*

- genesis
- generate
- **endo**genous — WITHIN
- **exo**genous — OUTSIDE
- **neuro**genesis — NERVE

PART 3 — *KIND*

- genre
- generic
- **carcino**genic — CANCER
- **hetero**geneous — DIFFERENT
- **homo**geneous — SAME

STUDY CARD 1 — gen – birth, race *GREEK*

genetics **(ics- study of)** the study of heredity and the variation of inherited characteristics.

gender - biologically, either of the two sexes at birth (male and female). Gender can also refer to **gender identity.**

pro**gen**y **(pro- forward)** to bring forth a descendant or offspring, such as a child, plant, or animal.

con**gen**ital **(con- together)** existing at or prior to birth. *congenital deafness

genocide **(cide- to kill)** the deliberate killing of a large group of people, especially those of a particular racial, cultural, or political group or nation.

STUDY CARD 2 — gen – origin, produce *GREEK*

genesis - the **origin** or coming into being of something. *the genesis of a new environmental movement.

generate - to **produce; to create**. *to generate ideas.

endo**gen**ous **(endo- inside)** produced or originating from within an organism. *endogenous gene sequences.

exo**gen**ous **(exo- outside)** produced or originating from outside an organism.

neuro**gen**esis **(neuro- nerve)** the growth and development of nerve tissue.

STUDY CARD 3 — gen - kind *GREEK*

genre - a kind, style, or category of art, literature, etc.

generic - relating to an entire kind, group or class; general *substituting generics for brand-name drugs

carcino**gen**ic **(carcino- cancer)** a substance or agent that causes cancer. *Which chemicals are known to cause cancer?

hetero**gen**ous **(hetero- different)** composed of parts of different kinds; different substances

homo**gen**ous **(homo-same)** composed of parts of same kind.

Quiz 21　　　　　　　　　Latin and Greek Word Roots

Part 1. Write the word for the definition.

| genetics | gender | congenital | genocide | progeny |

1. _____ the study of heredity and the variation of inherited characteristics.
2. _____ to bring forth a descendant or offspring, such as a child, plant, or animal.
3. _____ existing at or prior to birth
4. _____ the deliberate killing of a large group of people
5. _____ biologically, either of the two sexes at birth (male and female).

| exogenous | neurogenesis | genesis | generate | endogenous |

6. _____ the growth and development of nerve tissue.
7. _____ produced or originating from outside an organism.
8. _____ to produce; to create.
9. _____ the origin or coming into being of something.
10. _____ produced or originating from within an organism.

| genre | carcinogenic | generic | homogenous | heterogenous |

11. _____ composed of parts of same kind.
12. _____ a kind, style, or category of art, literature, etc.
13. _____ composed of parts of different kinds; different substances
14. _____ a substance or agent that causes cancer.
15. _____ relating to an entire kind, group or class; general

Part 2. Write the word root for each word.

| ics | pro | con | cide |

1. study _____ 2. to kill _____ 3. together _____ 4. forward _____

| endo | exo | neuro | carcino |

5. cancer _____ 6. outside _____ 7. inside _____ 8. nerve _____

| hetero | homo |

9. same _____ 10. different _____

pedestrian
pedicure
pedometer
pedal
peddle

WORD CHART LESSON 22

amphi**pod**
arthro**pod**
podium
podiatrist
anti**pod**es

pediatrics
pedology
ortho**ped**ics
pedagogue
pediatrician

LESSON 22

ped, pod

FOOT, FEET

ped

CHILD

PART 1 — *FOOT, FEET*

- **ped**estrian
- **ped**i|cur|e — CARE
- **ped**o|meter — MEASURE
- **ped**al
- **ped**dle

PART 2 — *FOOT, FEET*

- BOTH — amphi|**pod**
- JOINT — arthro|**pod**
- **pod**ium
- **pod**iatr|ist — ONE WHO
- AGAINST — anti|**pod**es

PART 3 — *CHILD*

- **ped**iatr|ics — HEALING / STUDY OF
- **ped**ology — STUDY OF
- CORRECT — ortho|**ped**ics
- **ped**agog|ue — LEADER
- **ped**iatr|ician — HEALING

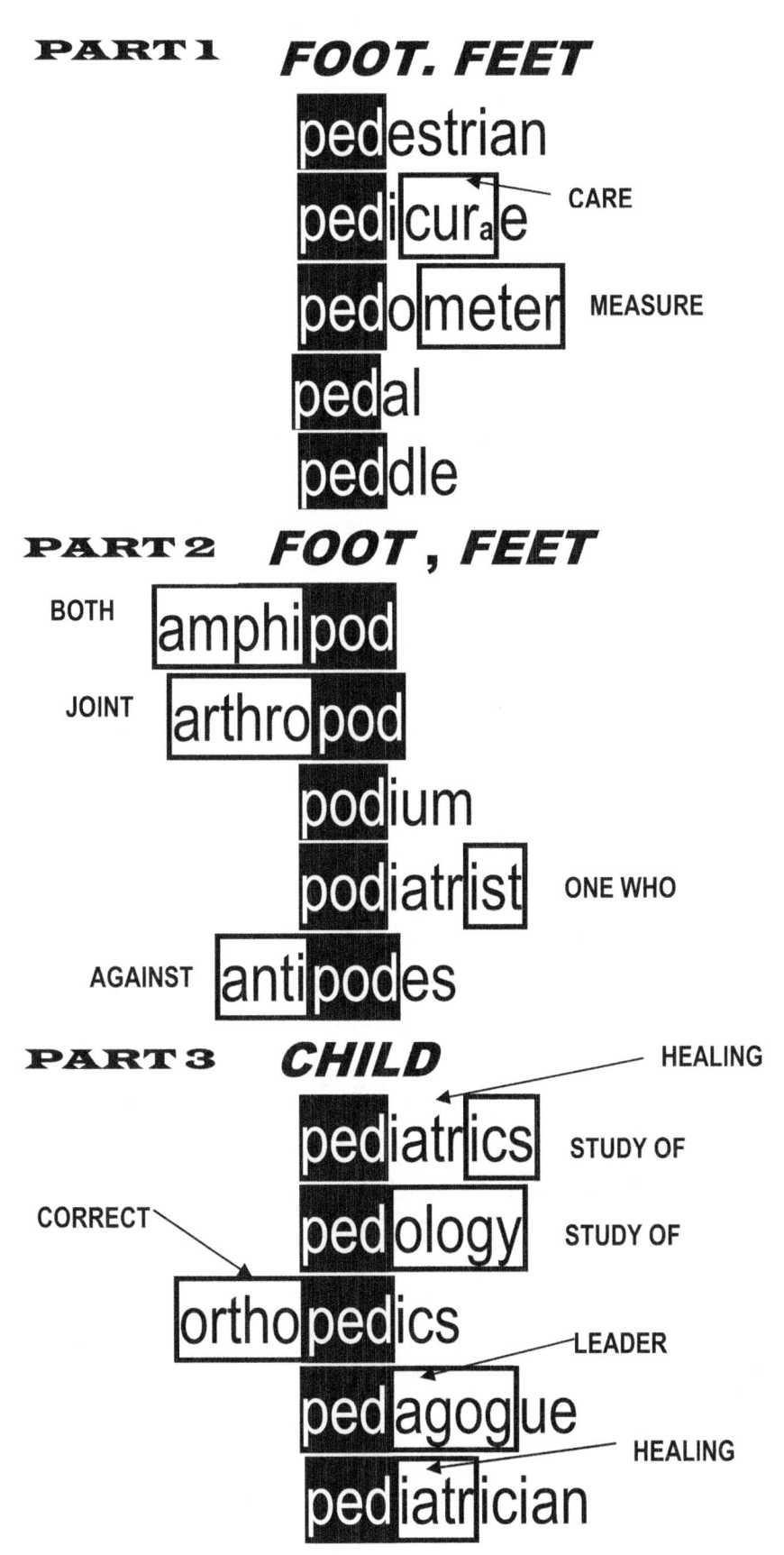

STUDY CARD 1 — ped – foot, feet — GREEK

pedestrian - 1.a person traveling on foot. 2.lacking inspiration or excitement; dull.

pedicure (cure- care) professional care of the feet and toenails.

pedometer (meter- measure) an instrument for measuring the distance traveled on foot by recording the number of steps taken.

pedals - foot-operated levers used for powering a bicycle or other vehicle propelled by the legs.

peddle - to sell something, (especially small goods) by walking from house to house or going from place to place.

STUDY CARD 2 — ped – foot, feet — GREEK

amphipod (amphi- both) crustaceans having legs for walking and for swimming.

arthropod (arthro- joint) invertebrate animals with jointed legs, an exoskeleton, and a segmented body.

podium - 1.a small platform on which a person may stand. 2.any structure resembling or functioning as a foot.

podiatrist (ist- one who) one who treats the feet and their ailments.

antipod**es** (anti- against) the parts of the earth diametrically opposite *such as Australia and New Zealand, as contrasted to the western hemisphere.

STUDY CARD 3 — ped – child — GREEK

pediatrics (iatr- healing) the branch of medicine dealing with children and their diseases.

pedology (logy- study of) the study of the behavior and development of children.

orthoped**ics** (ortho- correct) the branch of medicine dealing with correcting problems of the musculoskeletal system. (NOTE: not limited to children.)

pedagogue (agog- leader) a schoolteacher (leader), especially one who likes to teach people things in a firm, dogmatic. *a way as if they know more than anyone else.

pediatrician (iatr- healing) a doctor who specializes in the care of children.

Quiz 22   Latin and Greek Word Roots

Part 1. Write the word for the definition.

| pedestrian | pedometer | pedals | peddle | pedicure |

1. _____ professional care of the feet and toenails.
2. _____ a person traveling on foot.
3. _____ foot-operated levers.
4. _____ to sell something, (especially small goods) by walking.
5. _____ an instrument for measuring the distance traveled on foot

| podiatrist | arthropod | podium | antipodes | amphipod |

6. _____ one who treats the feet and their ailments.
7. _____ a small platform on which a person may stand.
8. _____ crustaceans having legs for walking and for swimming.
9. _____ invertebrate animals with jointed legs, an exoskeleton, and a segmented body.
10. _____ the **parts of the earth diametrically opposite** such as Australia and New Zealand, as contrasted to the western hemisphere.

| orthopedics | pediatrics | pedagogue | pedology | pediatrician |

11. _____ a doctor who specializes in the care of children.
12. _____ the branch of medicine dealing with children and their diseases.
13. _____ the study of the behavior and development of children.
14. _____ the branch of medicine dealing with correcting problems of the musculoskeletal system.
15. _____ a schoolteacher (leader), especially one who likes to teach people things in a firm, dogmatic

Part 2. Write the word root for each word.

| cure | meter | anti | amphi |

1 against _____   2. both _____   3. care _____   4. measure _____

| arthro | iatr | orth | agog |

5 joint _____   6. correct _____   7. healing _____   8. leader _____

an**arch**y
mon**arch**y
olig**arch**y
matri**arch**y
patri**arch**y

auto**cracy**
theo**cracy**
demo**cracy**
techno**cracy**
aristo**cracy**

architect
archipelago
archetype
protocol
protagonist

WORD CHART LESSON 23

LESSON 23

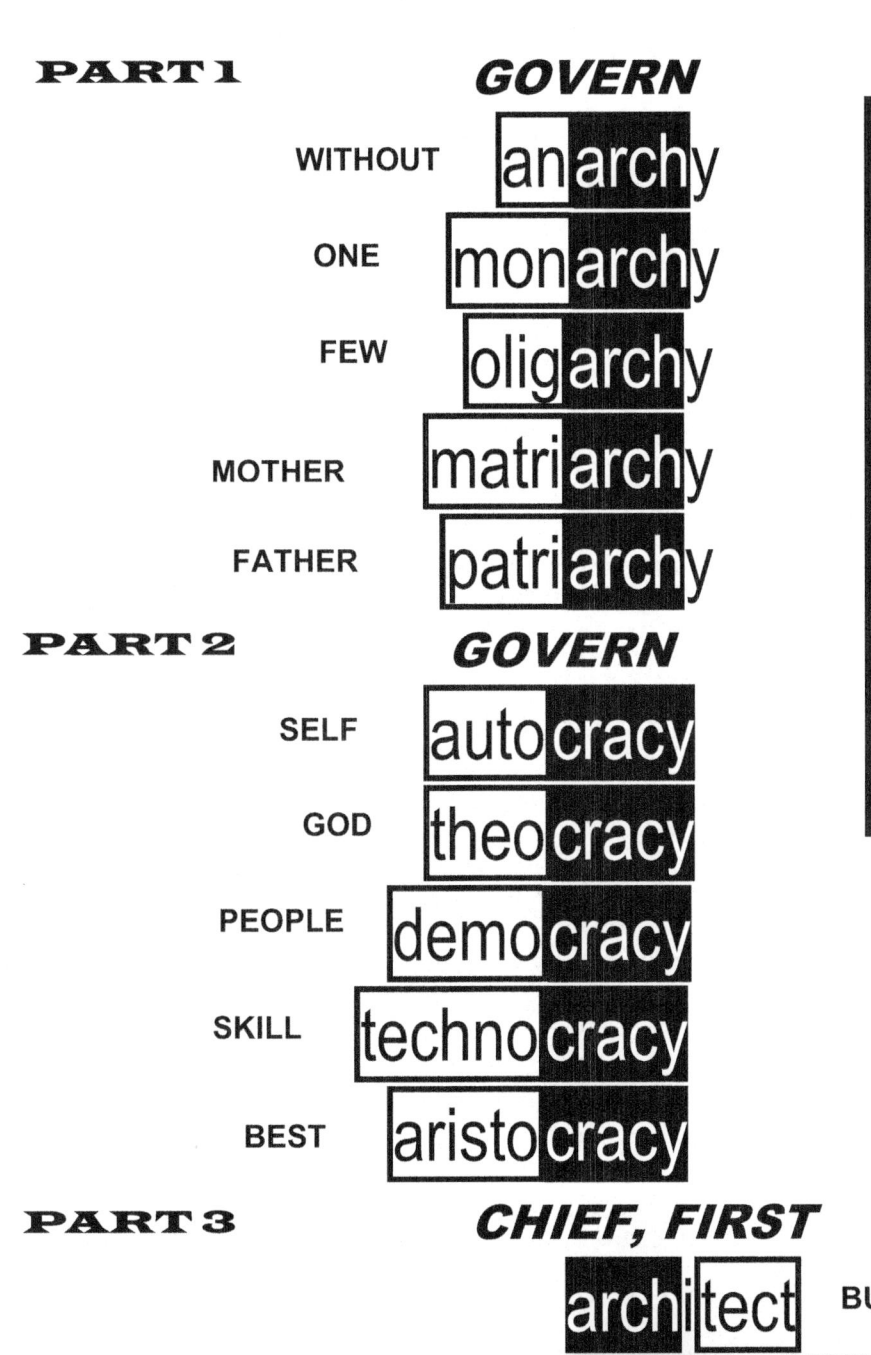

arch — GOVERN
cracy — GOVERN
arch/i/e — CHIEF, FIRST
prot/o — CHIEF, FIRST

PART 1 — GOVERN

- WITHOUT — **an**archy
- ONE — **mon**archy
- FEW — **olig**archy
- MOTHER — **matri**archy
- FATHER — **patri**archy

PART 2 — GOVERN

- SELF — **auto**cracy
- GOD — **theo**cracy
- PEOPLE — **demo**cracy
- SKILL — **techno**cracy
- BEST — **aristo**cracy

PART 3 — CHIEF, FIRST

- **archi**tect — BUILDER
- **archi**pelago(s) — SEA
- **arche**type
- **proto**col
- **prot**agonist(es) — ACTOR

STUDY CARD 1 — arch – rule, govern *(GREEK)*

anarchy (an- without) without rule; absence of government; lawlessness.

*After its ruler died, the country was in a state of anarchy.

monarch (mon- one) the one or sole ruler of a nation or state.

*A monarchy is a government controlled by a king or a ruler.

oligarchy (olig- few) a government having only a few rulers.

matriarch (matri- mother) the mother and ruler of a family or group of people.

patriarch (patri -father) the father and ruler of a family or group of people.

STUDY CARD 2 — cracy - govern *(GREEK)*

autocracy (auto- self) a country, state, or society governed by one person with absolute power.

theocracy (theo- God) a system of government in which Priests rule in the name of God or a god.

democracy (demo- people) government run by the people either directly or through elected officials. *The Greeks were the first society with a democracy.

technocracy (techno- skill) the government or control of society or industry by an elite of technical experts.

aristocracy (aris- best) govern by the elite or upper class; a class given special privileges because of birth, wealth, and nobility.

STUDY CARD 3 — arch/prot/o – chief, first *(GREEK)*

architect (tekton- builder) the chief designer or builder of buildings and other projects. *Who is the architect for the new bridge?

archipelago (pelego- sea) the chief islands; a sea or stretch of water containing many islands. *the Indonesian archipelago

archetype – the first model of a piece of work. *Henry Ford's assembly line was the archetype of the modern auto industry.

protocol – 1. the official procedure or system of rules governing affairs of state or diplomatic occasions. 2. an original first draft of a document.

protagonist (agonist- actor) the leading character or one of the major actors in a drama, movie, novel, or other fictional text.

Quiz 23 Latin and Greek Word Roots

Part 1. Write the word for the definition.

| anarchy | matriarch | monarch | oligarchy | patriarch |

1. _____ the mother and ruler of a family or group of people.
2. _____ the father and ruler of a family or group of people.
3. _____ without rule; absence of government; lawlessness.
4. _____ the one or sole ruler of a nation or state.
5. _____ a government having only a few rulers.

| theocracy | autocracy | democracy | aristocracy | technocracy |

6. _____ government run by the people either directly or through elected officials.
7. _____ a country, state, or society governed by one person with absolute power.
8. _____ govern by the elite or upper class
9. _____ a system of government in which Priests rule in the name of God or a god.
10. _____ the government or control of society or industry by an elite of technical experts.

| archetype | protocol | protagonist | archipelago | architect |

11. _____ the chief designer or builder of buildings and other projects.
12. _____ the chief islands; a sea or stretch of water containing many islands.
13. _____ the first model of a piece of work.
14. _____ the leading character or one of the major actors in a drama, movie, novel, or other fictional text.
15. _____ the official procedure or system of rules governing affairs of state or diplomatic occasions.

Part 2. Write the word root for each word.

| pelego | olig | matri | patri |

1 father _____ 2. sea _____ 3. few _____ 4. mother _____

| demo | techno | aris | agonist |

5 actor _____ 6. skill _____ 7. best _____ 8. people _____

descend
denounce
depose
demote
devaluate

depress
despondent
decelerate
degenerate
debilitate

deter
deflect
detract
depredation
defer

WORD CHART LESSON 24

PART 1 ***DOWN***

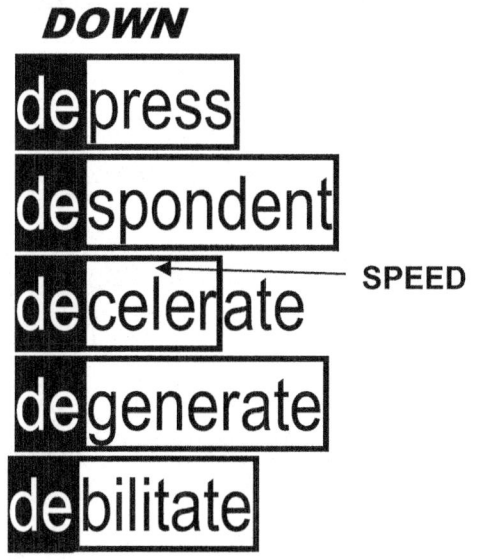

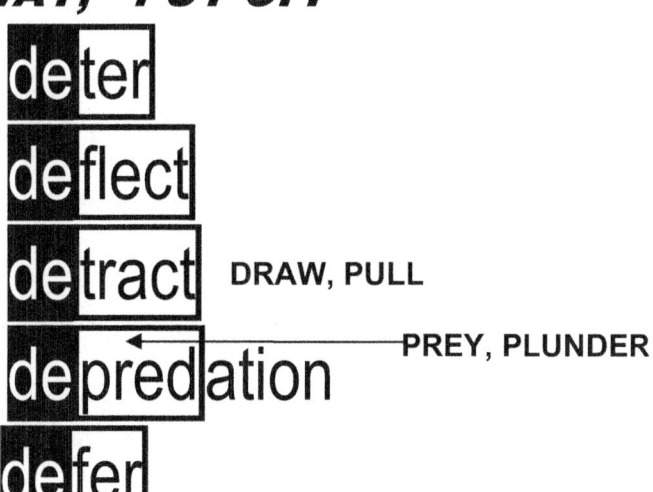

- **de**scend — CLIMB
- **de**nounce
- **de**pose — PUT, PLACE
- **de**mote — MOVE
- **de**valuate

LESSON 24

de
DOWN
AWAY
OFF

PART 2 ***DOWN***

- **de**press
- **de**spondent
- **de**celerate — SPEED
- **de**generate
- **de**bilitate

PART 3 ***AWAY, *PUT OFF***

- **de**ter
- **de**flect
- **de**tract — DRAW, PULL
- **de**pred*ation* — PREY, PLUNDER
- *****de**fer

STUDY CARD 1   **de – down**   LATIN

descend (scend- climb) to climb down.

denounce - to put down; to condemn openly, publicly, to be wrong or evil.
*The assembly denounced the use of violence.

depose (pos- put, place) to put down; to remove from an office or position, especially high office: *The people deposed the dictator.

demote (mot- move) to move down: to reduce to a lower grade, rank, class, or position (opposed to promote): They demoted the careless waiter to busboy.

devaluate – take down or lessen in value.

STUDY CARD 2   **de – down**   LATIN

depress – to press down.

despondent – down; depressed; discouraged; loss of hope or courage. *He grew more and more despondent.

decelerate (celer- speed) is to slow down; to accelerate is to speed up.

degenerate - to fall below a normal or desirable level in physical, mental, or moral qualities; deteriorate: *The morale of the soldiers degenerated.

debilitate – to weaken; to **impair the strength of; enfeeble.** *His weaknesses debilitate him despite his overwhelming physical might.

STUDY CARD 3   **de – away, put off**   LATIN

deter - to prevent; to keep from doing something.

deflect - draw away; turn aside. *to deflect our attention from what was happening

detract - pull away; diminish the worth or value of (a quality or achievement).
His attitude in no way detracts from his achievement.

depredation (pred- prey, plunder) the act of preying upon or plundering; robbery.
*protecting grain from the depredations of rats and mice.

defer - put off (an action or event) to a later time; postpone. *They deferred the decision until they heard from all the witnesses.

Quiz 24 — Latin and Greek Word Roots

Part 1. Write the word for the definition.

| devaluate | descend | denounce | demote | depose |

1. _____ take down or lessen in value.
2. _____ to put down; to condemn openly publicly declare to be wrong or evil.
3. _____ to climb down.
4. _____ to put down; to remove from an office or position, especially high office:
5. _____ to move down: to reduce to a lower grade, rank, class, or position

| despondent | debilitate | degenerate | decelerate | depress |

6. _____ down; depressed; discouraged; loss of hope or courage.
7. _____ to weaken; to **impair the strength of; enfeeble.**
8. _____ to press down.
9. _____ to slow down; to accelerate is to speed up.
10. _____ to fall below a normal or desirable level in physical, mental, or moral qualities; deteriorate

| deter | detract | deflect | defer | depredation |

11. _____ to prevent; to keep from doing something.
12. _____ diminish the worth or value of (a quality or achievement).
13. _____ draw away; turn aside.
14. _____ the act of preying upon or plundering; robbery.
15. _____ put off (an action or event) to a later time; postpone.

Part 2. Write the word root for each word.

| scend | pos | celer | mot |

1. speed _____   2. climb _____   3. move _____   4. put, place _____

WORD CHART LESSON 25

digress
diverse
disrupt
distinguish
discriminate

disparate
dispassionate
dissent
diffident
disseminate

redundant
reciprocate
recapitulate
retract
remorse

LESSON 25

di
dis
NOT
APART

re
BACK, AGAIN

PART 1 *APART*

- **di**gress — STEP, GO
- **di**verse
- **dis**rupt — BREAK
- **dis**tinguish
- **dis**criminate

PART 2 *NOT, *APART*

- **dis**parate — EQUAL
- **dis**passionate
- **dis**sent — FEEL
- **dif**fident — FAITH
- ***dis**seminate

PART 3 *AGAIN, *BACK*

- **re**dundant
- **re**ciprocate
- **re**capitulate
- ***re**tract — DRAW, PULL
- ***re**morse

103

STUDY CARD 1   **di, dis – apart**   LATIN

digress (gress- step, go) step apart; to go off the subject.

diverse being apart; composed of different elements: variety. *different types of people (such as people of **different** races or cultures) in a group or organization.

disrupt (rupt- break) to break apart; rupture. to throw into disorder. *demonstrators trying to disrupt a meeting.

distinguish to tell apart; to cause to stand out.

discriminate - to tell apart; to see the difference and make a clear distinction. *Babies can discriminate between different facial expressions.

STUDY CARD 2   **dis – not, apart**   LATIN

disparate (par- equal) not the same; different; unequal. *things so unlike that there is no basis for comparison.

dispassionate - without passion; not influenced by strong emotion, rational and impartial. *She dealt with life's problems in a calm, dispassionate way.

dissent (sent- feel) a strong feeling against; a difference of opinion. *often about an official suggestion… a protest against government policies.

diffident (fid- faith) not having faith in oneself; a person who is shy, has no self-confidence.

disseminate – to scatter apart; to make widely known.

STUDY CARD 3   **re – again, back**   LATIN

redundant - saying again and again; wordy and repetitive; unnecessary.

reciprocate - respond again (to a gesture or action) by making a corresponding one. *The favor was reciprocated.

recapitulate - to say again in a different way; make a summary.

retract – (tract- draw, pull) to pull back; to withdraw

remorse - deep regret or guilt for a wrong committed.

*They were filled with remorse and shame.

Quiz 25   Latin and Greek Word Roots

Part 1. Write the word for the definition.

| digress | distinguish | disrupt | discriminate | diverse |

1. _____ to break apart; rupture. to throw into disorder.
2. _____ to cause to stand out.
3. _____ to see the difference and make a clear distinction.
4. _____ being apart; composed of different elements: variety.
5. _____ to go off the subject.

| diffident | disseminate | disparate | dispassionate | dissent |

6. _____ to scatter apart; to make widely known
7. _____ not having faith in oneself; a person who is shy, has no self-confidence.
8. _____ a strong feeling against; a difference of opinion.
9. _____ without passion; not influenced by strong emotion, rational and impartial.
10. _____ not the same; different; unequal.

| redundant | reciprocate | recapitulate | retract | remorse |

11. _____ deep regret or guilt for a wrong committed.
12. _____ to pull back; to withdraw
13. _____ to say again in a different way; make a summary.
14. _____ respond again (to a gesture or action) by making a corresponding one.
15. _____ saying again and again; wordy and repetitive; unnecessary.

Part 2. Write the word root for each word.

| fid | sent | par | rupt |

1 faith _____ 2. break _____ 3. equal _____ 4. feel _____

| gress | dis | re | tract |

5 draw, pull _____ 6. step, go _____ 7. not, apart _____ 8. back, again _____

Final Examination

DIRECTIONS: Match the word on the left to its meaning on the right, Write the letter for the answer.

TEST 1 (LESSONS 1, 2)

(g) 1. cartography   a. beautiful writing

2. cryptography   b. correct spelling

3. calligraphy   c. study of different races

4. orthography   d. breaking secret codes

5. ethnology   e. study of the solid earth

6. cosmology   f. study of causes; diseases

7. etiology   g. map making

8. geology   h. study of the universe

TEST 2 (LESSONS 3, 4)

1. apathy   a. extra, unnecessary

2. emigrate   b. to infer

3. extemporaneous   c. without rule; lawlessness

4. extrapolate   d. little or no preparation

5. extraneous   e. public speaking or reading

6. elocution   f. not harmful; uninspiring

7. innocuous   g. to move out

8. anarchy   h. without feeling or emotion

Copyright 2020, Matthew Glavach, Ph.D.

TEST 3 (LESSONS 5, 6)

1. superfluous
2. supercilious
3. debacle
4. debilitate
5. provident
6. predecessor
7. premonition
8. subversive

a. sudden breakdown; complete failure
b. to weaken
c. someone, something that came before.
d. a feeling; warning of danger to come
e. to turn on; to undermine
f. acting superior or pompous
g. to see before; prudent
h. overflowing; beyond what is needed

TEST 4 (LESSONS 7, 8)

1. transient
2. transaction
3. transgress
4. dialogue
5. ductile
6. intransigent
7. concede
8. intercede

a. to conduct or negotiate; business affairs
b. written and spoken communication
c. someone passing through
d. not willing to compromise
e. to surrender or yield
f. to go between; to mediate
g. easily led or persuaded; gullible
h. to step across between good and evil

TEST 5 (LESSONS 9, 10)

1. symphony
2. coalesce
3. collusion
4. speculation
5. introspection
6. synthesis
7. conspicuous
8. perspicacious

a. unite
b. standing out
c. guess at how something is going to come out
d. intelligent; observant
e. self-examination
f. harmony of sounds and colors
g. putting things together into a meaningful whole
h. secret or illegal cooperation

TEST 6 (LESSONS 11, 12)

1. circumspect
2. peripheral
3. pervade
4. egocentric
5. benevolent
6. benign
7. euthanasia
8. benediction

a. spread or diffuse throughout; permeate
b. not harmful.
c. intentionally ending a life
d. **cautious**
e. kindness and good will
f. an **invocation; to say a blessing**
g. **an outer boundary;** a secondary interest
h. self-centered

TEST 7 (LESSONS 13, 14)

1. pseudonym   a. a beginner; novice
2. neophyte   b. to make harmful statements
3. novel   c. not a good place
4. neologism   d. a curse
5. misogynist   e. a false name
6. malediction   f. newly coined word or expression
7. malign   g. one **who hates mistreats women**
8. dystopia   h. new; fresh; original

TEST 8 (LESSONS 15, 16)

1. dialogue   a. a section or speech at the end
2. bilingual   b. speak two languages
3. prologue   c. part that comes before; introduction
4. epilogue   d. to draw a line around; encircle
5. ideography   e. a conversation
6. circumscribe   f. the written text of a play, movie
7. script   g. words having the same first consonant
8. alliteration   h. graphic symbols

TEST 9 (LESSONS 17, 18)

1. advocate
2. indict
3. colloquial
4. loquacious
5. abdicate
6. equivocal
7. provocative
8. evoke

a. charge with a serious crime
b. renounce one's throne
c. talkative; wordy
d. more than one meaning; deceive or mislead
e. **excite, or stimulate**
f. recall to the conscious mind
g. speaking together informally
h. in favor of something

TEST 10 (LESSONS 19, 20)

1. biotic
2. vivacious
3. bioluminescence
4. fable
5. affable
6. xenophobia
7. philosopher
8. bibliophile

a. living organisms that produce light
b. short story, often with animals speaking
c. great love of books
d. lively and spirited; animated
e. relating to life
f. has great wisdom
g. prejudice; people from other countries
h. friendly, good-natured

TEST 11 (LESSONS 21, 22)

1. homogenous
2. carcinogenic
3. peddle
4. podiatrist
5. pedagogue
6. pediatrician
7. congenital
8. genesis

a. to sell something
b. one who treats the feet
c. **origin of something**
d. **the care of children**
e. **causes cancer**
f. existing at or prior to birth
g. a schoolteacher (leader)
h. parts of same kind

TEST 12 (LESSONS 23, 24)

1. anarchy
2. archipelago
3. aristocracy
4. denounce
5. despondent
6. debilitate
7. deter
8. deflect

a. the chief islands
b. to prevent
c. to condemn openly
d. lawlessness
e. weaken, **enfeeble**
f. govern by the elite or upper class
g. depressed; discouraged
h. draw away; turn aside

TEST 13 (LESSON 25)

1. remorse
2. redundant
3. disseminate
4. dissent
5. disparate
6. discriminate
7. distinguish
8. digress

a. make widely known
b. go off the subject
c. no basis for comparison
d. see the difference
e. deep regret or guilt
f. cause to stand out
g. strong feeling against
h. wordy and repetitive

LESSON QUIZZES. ANSWER KEY

QUIZ 1, PART 1: (Word/Definition)
1. geology	2. exobiology	3. ecology	4. etiology	5. biology
6. genealogy	7. chronology	8. zoology	9. psychology	10. astrology
11. ethnology	12. audiology	13. cosmology	14. anthropology	15. paleoanthropology

QUIZ 1, PART 2: (Word Root)
1. bio	2. etio	3. geo	4. exo	5. eco
6. astro	7. psych	8. genea	9. chron	10. zo
11. cosm	12. ethn	13. paleo	14. anthrop	15. audi

QUIZ 2, PART 1: (Word/Definition)
1. biography	2. autobiography	3. bibliography	4. monograph	5. choreography
6. orthography	7. calligraphy	8. geography	9. cartography	10. demography
11. chronograph	12. autograph	13. cryptography	14. electroencephalograph	
15. electrocardiograph				

QUIZ, PART 2: (Word Root)
1. bio	2. crypto	3. auto	4. ortho	5. biblio
6. geo	7. carto	8. demo	9. choreo	10. calli
11. auto	12. cardio	13. chron	14. auto	15. encephalo

QUIZ 3, PART 1: (Word/Definition)
1. evacuate	2. emissary	3. emancipate	4. elocution	5. emigrate
6. extol	7. extemporaneous	8. extricate	9. exonerate	10. exclude
11. extrovert	12. extraordinary	13. extraterrestrial	14. extraneous	15. extrapolate

QUIZ 3, PART 2: (Word Root)
1. terr	2. vert	3. clud	4. ex	5. trica
6. migr	7. vacu	8. miss	9. out	10. locu

QUIZ 4, PART 1: (Word/Definition)
1. amorphous	2. apathy	3. atheist	4. amnesia	5. atrophy
6. anonymous	7. anarchy	8. anorexia	9. anesthesia	10. anemia
11. immortal	12. incredulous	13. innocuous	14. irreversible	15. illiterate

QUIZ 4, PART 2: (Word Root)
1. pathy	2. mne	3. onym	4. the	5. trophy
6. mort	7. liter	8. esthes	9. emia	10. orexia
11. re	12. voc	13. noc	14. cred	15. liter

QUIZ 5, PART 1: (Word/Definition)
1. premonition	2. precursor	3. precaution	4. precocious	5. precursor
6. prognosis	7. prologue	8. improvise	9. provident	10. procrastinate
11. postnatal	12. posterity	13. posterior	14. posthumous	15. postlude

QUIZ 5, PART 2: (Word Root)
1. log	2. caut	3. pre	4. mon	5. gnos
6. humus	7. nat	8. vid, vis	9. lud	10. cras

QUIZ 6, PART 1: (Word/Definition)
1. degenerate	2. descend	3. decelerate	4. debacle	5. debilitate
6. subterranean	7. subversive	8. sublingual	9. subjugate	10. subordinate
11. supervisor	12. superlative	13. superfluous	14. supercilious	15. superstitious

QUIZ 6, PART 2: (Word Root)
1. scend	2. vers	3. ord	4. terr	5. celer
6. sub	7. vis	8. flu	9. super	10. de

QUIZ 7, PART 1: (Word/Definition)
  1. precede   2. exceed   3. recede   4. intercede   5. concede
  6. ductile   7. seduce   8. conduct   9. induct   10. aqueduct
  11. conclude   12. seclude   13. preclude   14. inconclusive   15. exclusive
QUIZ 7 PART 2: (Word Root)
  1. pre   2. inter   3. ex   4. re
  5. se   6. aqu   7. con   8. con
  9. in   10. clud, clus   11. duct   12. cede

QUIZ 8, PART 1: (Word/Definition)
  1. dialogue   2. diagnosis   3. dialectic   4. diaphanous   5. diameter
  6. transaction   7. transfer   8. transgress   9. transparent   10. transport
  11. transient   12. intransigent   13. transition   14. transcend   15. translucent
QUIZ 8, PART 2: (Word Root)
  1. phan   2. gnos   3. log   4. meter
  5. port   6. act   7. gress   8. par

QUIZ 9 PART 1: (Word/Definition)
  1. synthesis   2. asynchronous   3. synchronize   4. idiosyncrasy   5. syllable
  6. symphony   7. symbiosis   8. sympathy   9. symposium   10. syntax
  11. collaborate   12. coalesce   13. collusion   14. congregate   15. confluence
QUIZ 9, PART 2: (Word Root)
  1. onym   2. chron   3. the   4. lable
  5. phon   6. ideo   7. pathy   8. tax
  9. greg   10. flu   11. pos   12. bio

QUIZ 10, PART 1: (Word/Definition)
  1. perspective   2. specter   3. circumspect   4. introspection   5. speculation
  6. vista   7. visible   8. evident   9. provident   10. visionary
  11. telescope   12. conspicuous   13. auspicious   14. horoscope   15. perspicacious
QUIZ 10, PART 2: (Word Root)
  1. per   2. in   3. ible   4. circumn
  6. tele   7. horo   8. e   9. con

QUIZ 11, PART 1: (Word/Definition)
  1. circumvent   2. circumambulate 3. circumspect   4. circumference   5. circumlocution
  6. pervade   7. periscope   8. peripheral   9. perianth   10. peripatetic
  11. central   12. concentrate   13. concentric   14. eccentric   15. egocentric
QUIZ 11, PART 2: (Word Root)
  1. scop   2. vad   3. vent   4. anth
  5. ambul   6. spect   7. locu   8. ego

QUIZ 12, PART 1: (Word/Definition)
  1. benefactress   2. benevolent   3. beneficial   4. benefactor   5. beneficiary
  6. bon vivant   7. benign   8. bona fida   9. benediction   10. beneficent
  11. euphemism   12. euphoria   13. eulogy   14. euthanasia   15. eugenics
QUIZ 12, PART 2: (Word Root)
  1. dict   2. fic   3. fida   4. ess
  5. phem   6. thanas   7. phor   8. viv

QUIZ 13, PART 1: (Word/Definition)
 1. malign   2. malaria   3. malodorous   4. malevolent   5. malediction
 6. misology   7. misogamist   8. misandry   9. misanthrope 10. misogynist
 11. dyspepsia   12. dyslexia   13. dystopia   14. dystrophy   15. dysgraphia
QUIZ 13, PART 2: (Word Root)
 1. lex   2. speak   3. andr   4. trophy
 5. gyn   6. log   7. peps   8. gam

QUIZ 14, PART 1: (Word/Definition)
 1. monomial   2. ignominy   3. nomenclature 4. nominate   5. misnomer
 6. antonym   7. pseudonym   8. anonymous   9. homonym   10. synonym
 11. novel   12. innovate   13. neonatal   14. neophyte   15. neologism
QUIZ 14, PART 2: (Word Root)
 1. syn   2. mis   3. nov   4. ig
 5. pseudo   6. homo   7. an   8. anti
 9. log   10. phyte   11. mon   12. nat

QUIZ 15, PART 1: (Word/Definition)
 1. circumscribe 2. prescribe   3. inscribe   4. describe   5. scribe
 6. manuscript   7. script   8. transcript   9. scriptorium 10. Scripture
 11. lexicography 12. ideography 13. graphology 14. graphics   15. monograph
QUIZ 15, PART 2: (Word Root)
 1. in   2. scrib   3. pre   4. de
 5. manu   6. trans   7. orium   8. circum
 9. ideo   10. ology   11. mono   12. lex

QUIZ 16, PART 1: (Word/Definition)
 1. unilingual   2. linguist   3. bilingual   4. lingual   5. linguistics
 6. trilogy   7. monologue   8. epilogue   9. prologue   10. dialogue
 11. literate   12. literary   13. illiterate 14. alliteration 15. literature
QUIZ 16, PART 2: (Word Root)
 1. ist   2. uni   3. ics   4. bi
 5. epi   6. mono   7. pro   8. dia

QUIZ 17, PART 1: (Word/Definition)
 1. dictate   2. dictator   3. indict   4. jurisdiction 5. abdicate
 6. valedictorian 7. edict   8. verdict   9. dictum   10. contradict
 11. elocution   12. circumlocution 13. colloquial 14. loquacious 15. soliloquy
QUIZ 17, PART 2: (Word Root)
 1. ab   2. ver   3. juris   4. or
 5. circum   6. soli   7. vale   8. contra

QUIZ 18, PART 1: (Word/Definition)
 1. symphony   2. cacophony   3. telephone   4. megaphone   5. euphony
 6. irrevocable 7. advocate   8. equivocal   9. convocation 10. vocation
 11. evoke   12. provocative 13. revoke   14. convoke   15. invoke
QUIZ 18, PART 2: (Word Root)
 1. eu   2. tele   3. sym   4. mega
 5. ir   6. caco   7. equi   8. con
 9. re   10. phon   11. pro   12. voc

QUIZ 19, PART 1: (Word/Definition)
1. bibliophile
2. philology
3. philanthropist
4. philatelist
5. philosopher
6. hydrophobia
7. arachnophobia
8. acrophobia
9. xenophobia
10. agoraphobia
11. affable
12. fable
13. ineffable
14. infamous
15. fame

QUIZ 19, PART 2: (Word Root)
1. acro
2. biblio
3. anthrop
4. soph
5. hydro
6. arachno
7. xeno
8. agora

QUIZ 20, PART 1: (Word/Definition)
1. biotic
2. biology
3. abiotic
4. biome
5. amphibian
6. symbiosis
7. autobiography
8. biography
9. bioluminescence
10. biodegradable
11. survive
12. revive
13. viviparous
14. ovoviviparous
15. vivacious

QUIZ 20, PART 2: (Word Root)
1. ome
2. logy
3. sym
4. amphi
5. graph
6. grad
7. de
8. sur
9. ovo
10. re
11. viv, bio
12. parous

QUIZ 21, PART 1: (Word/Definition)
1. genetics
2. progeny
3. congenital
4. genocide
5. gender
6. neurogenesis
7. exogenous
8. generate
9. genesis
10. endogenous
11. homogenous
12. genre
13. heterogenous
14. carcinogenic
15. generic

QUIZ 21, PART 2: (Word Root)
1. ics
2. cide
3. con
4. pro
5. carcino
6. exo
7. endo
8. neuro
9. homo
10. hetero

QUIZ 22, PART 1: (Word/Definition)
1. pedicure
2. pedestrian
3. pedals
4. peddle
5. pedometer
6. podiatrist
7. podium
8. amphipod
9. arthropod
10. antipodes
11. pediatrician
12. pediatrics
13. pedology
14. orthopedics
15. pedagogue

QUIZ 22, PART 2: (Word Root)
1. anti
2. amphi
3. cure
4. meter
5. arthro
6. ortho
7. iatr
8. agog

QUIZ 23, PART 1: (Word/Definition)
1. matriarch
2. patriarch
3. anarchy
4. monarch
5. oligarchy
6. democracy
7. autocracy
8. aristocracy
9. theocracy
10. technocracy
11. architect
12. archipelago
13. archetype
14. protagonist
15. protocol

QUIZ 23, PART 2: (Word Root)
1. patri
2. pelago
3. olig
4. matri
5. agonist
6. techno
7. aris
8. dem

QUIZ 24, PART 1: (Word/Definition)
1. devaluate
2. denounce
3. descend
4. depose
5. demote
6. despondent
7. debilitate
8. depress
9. decelerate
10. degenerate
11. deter
12. detract
13. deflect
14. depredation
15. defer

QUIZ 24, PART 2: (Word Root)
1. celer
2. scend
3. mot
4. pos

QUIZ 25, PART 1: (Word/Definition)
1. disrupt
2. distinguish
3. discriminate
4. diverse
5. digress
6. disseminate
7. diffident
8. dissent
9. dispassionate
10. disparate
11. remorse
12. retract
13. recapitulate
14. reciprocate
15. redundant

QUIZ 25, PART 2: (Word Root)
1. fid
2. rupt
3. par
4. sent
5. tract
6. gress
7. dis
8. re

FINAL EXAMINATION. ANSWER KEY.

(EXAM 1)   1. g   2. d   3. a   4. b   5. c   6. h   7. f   8. e

(EXAM 2)   1. h   2. g   3. d   4. b   5. a   6. e   7. f   8. c

(EXAM 3)   1. h   2. f   3. a   4. b   5. g   6. c   7. d   8. e

(EXAM 4)   1. c   2. a   3. h   4. b   5. g   6. d   7. e   8. f

(EXAM 5)   1. f   2. a   3. h   4. c   5. e   6. g   7. b   8. d

(EXAM 6)   1. d   2. g   3. a   4. h   5. e   6. b   7. c   8. f

(EXAM 7)   1. e   2. a   3. h   4. f   5. g   6. d   7. b   8. c

(EXAM 8)   1. e   2. b   3. c   4. a   5. h   6. d   7. f   8. g

(EXAM 9)   1. h   2. a   3. g   4. c   5. b   6. d   7. e   8. f

(EXAM 10)   1. e   2. d   3. a   4. b   5. h   6. g   7. f   8. c

(EXAM 11)   1. h   2. e   3. a   4. b   5. g   6. d   7. f   8. c

(EXAM 12)   1. d   2. a   3. f   4. c   5. g   6. e   7. b   8. h

(EXAM 13)   1. e   2. h   3. a   4. g   5. c   6. d   7. f   8. b

Printed in Great Britain
by Amazon